The Memorial Box

Linny Lee Saunders

*Retelling the stories of God's
faithfulness for future generations.*

Silver Lake Publisher
3655 W. Anthem Way
Suite A 109, #305
Phoenix, AZ 85086

A portion of the author's royalties will be donated to
"Ruby's Friends" @ *InternationalVoiceOfTheOrphan.com*
Ruby's Friends was created to care for medical needs of orphans
and vulnerable children in developing countries. Donations to
care for orphans and vulnerable children can be made at
InternationalVoiceOfTheOrphan.com.

International Standard Book Number: ISBN- 0692916733

Contents

To my grandtreasures:
Finley Asiimwee Lane,
Charlotte Rose,
Theodore Dwight,
Stone Wolfer Moon,
William Hudson,
Indio Wilde Gard,
Everlly Rain Elizabeth,
Sawyer Archer Len,
and
all the little ones yet to come…

Throughout my life Mimi has reveled in seasons of crazy joy, incredible favor and countless blessings as God has surprised me with the most incredible gifts (like you!). But Mimi has also had seasons of deep pain, indescribable heartache and unexpected loss. Regardless of the season, whether joyful or sorrowful, Jesus has always been astoundingly faithful to me. I pray that each of you know Jesus as your best friend and that you learn to walk with Him as I have! Walking with the Lord has brought me comfort, joy, love, strength and incredible peace. And I can say with complete confidence, my astoundingly faithful God has never failed me – not even once! I love you all so very much and I miss you every single day.

-Mimi

The

Memorial Box

Linny Lee Saunders

Chapter 1

"It's My Liver"

"It's my liver."

My eyes widened and my heart began to race wildly as fear gripped my soul. The text was from my husband, Dwight, who had been having a myriad of tests done in the Emergency Room at the University of Iowa. Normally I would have been with Dwight in the ER as they ran the tests, however, I was actually sitting on the opposite side of the *same* hospital with our 5 year-old, Isaiah, who had just had surgery.

Truthfully, I'm not really sure what I was expecting the results of Dwight's tests to show, but I definitely wasn't prepared for his text to say: "It's my liver."

Just a few days before my husband Dwight and I had driven over 1,200 miles to Iowa City for our son, Isaiah, to have a very delicate surgery performed by a

6

world-renowned surgeon. We had also brought our 10-year-old, Liberty, along as she was Isaiah's best bud and we were hoping her presence would make the whole trip easier on him.

In fact the month leading up to leaving for Isaiah's surgery had been a crazy whirlwind. It had started with Dwight and our daughter Emma co-leading a two-week mission trip to Africa. Flying home with the team, Dwight had begun not feeling well. At first we thought he had a virus. But after a few days home, he still wasn't better. In fact he seemed to be growing worse! He was vomiting often, very sleepy and had begun to lose weight.

In the meantime, our oldest son Tyler had called to say that while deployed he had realized how short life can be and decided he was coming home on leave to marry his high school sweetheart. He had asked beautiful Sarah over the phone, she had said yes, and they would be married the following week. He also asked Dwight to be his best man. A family wedding - we were all thrilled!

With Tyler's upcoming wedding, Dwight needed to be well so he went to see our doctor. The doctor ran a few routine tests and said that although his numbers did seem a tad off, he wasn't really concerned and sent Dwight home.

Yet Dwight continued to grow sicker! Tyler had now arrived home, and Dwight was spending every day in bed. This was so unlike him and I was growing very, very concerned!

Our son, Tyler, is rarely able to come home and here was dad, his best man, barely making an appearance. Dwight always loves being in the thick of each activity but instead he was in our room vomiting or sleeping the entire time. He was also continuing to lose weight.

Since Dwight's symptoms were only worsening, he returned to the doctor and, again, was told that although his numbers were still off, they weren't alarming. Of course we thought his weight loss alone was telling us otherwise!

All too soon the festivities were over, our son and his sweet bride left to honeymoon and it was time for us to leave for Isaiah's surgery in Iowa City.

The original plan had been for Dwight and I to take Isaiah together. But in the back of my mind all I could think of was how sick Dwight was and how hard it would be for him to ride 1,200 miles to Iowa City. Of course our little guy would be still recovering from extensive surgery on the way home and I couldn't imagine driving the 1,200 miles with a post-surgery Isaiah and a very sick husband.

I urged Dwight to stay home. But he didn't want me traveling that distance alone. Although I was grateful for his concern for me, I was really worried about him! What was wrong with him? Why did the doctor seem to think it was no big deal? In the end, Dwight had been insistent and had traveled with us.

So here we were in Iowa City, Isaiah had had his surgery the day before and Dwight and Liberty had spent the night in the Ronald McDonald house near the hospital. As they were on their way up to Isaiah's room Dwight had phoned me from the hospital parking garage to say he had been vomiting so much he felt he was too weak to get up to Isaiah's room. I insisted that I would come get Liberty from him and he would head straight to the ER! I asked our nurse to sit with Isaiah as I dashed down to meet them at the hospital entrance.

I will never forget how awful Dwight looked. My once tall, strong, dashingly handsome husband was bent part way over, his yellowed skin hanging on his thinner-than-should-ever-be body. He'd lost 30 pounds in just three weeks! I felt sick to my stomach looking at him. Something must be horribly wrong!

In all the flurry of activity, with the wedding and grown kids coming home I just hadn't really stopped to look at him and now that I had, I hated to admit it, but he looked like he was on death's door. We had to get to the bottom of this. I was comforted that we were at a major hospital.

Back upstairs and settled in Isaiah's hospital room with both Isaiah and Liberty, Dwight and I began texting as he navigated the Emergency Room process. He had sent several texts over the hour or so and then this:

"It's my liver."

Immediately nausea swept through my body, my heart started to race and fear overcame me. In that instant, thoughts swirled with every horrific possibility I could imagine: What would we do? Would Dwight ever even go home with us? We were about 1200 miles from home! Isaiah had just had surgery! We also had our nine-year-old with us. I knew no one nearby! Was it liver cancer? What could it be? How could he lose 30 pounds in three weeks? How did the doctor in our hometown not pick this up? What was going to happen? How would I get Isaiah and Liberty home?

And in that moment, with every imaginable scary thought freaking me out, nausea overwhelming me, and my heart beating wildly, suddenly, out of nowhere a steady stream of trinkets paraded through my mind. Each small trinket was from our **Memorial Box**: a small heart monitor lead, a little plastic shark, a rock, a toy mountain lion, a little log home, a teeny Radio Flyer wagon, an hour glass, and one by one I began to remember.

As each image passed by, the Lord whispered ever so gently to my soul, "Remember what each of these represent? Did I ever leave you during any of the situations that they stand for? I will not leave you now. I am right here and I am providing for every single thing you will need."

Instantly peace that could only come from Christ, flooded through my entire being and replaced the enormous dread, panic and fear that had moved in to my soul to torment me! Did His whispers mean that everything with Dwight's health would turn out perfectly? Well no, they didn't. But God's peace did mean that whatever the days ahead would hold, He was already there, meeting every single need we would have! He had this and I could trust Him.

Hard to imagine with our frail, human minds, yet the God of the Universe was more than aware that we were 1200 miles from home, we knew no one, one little son was recovering from extensive surgery, another young daughter with us, our other kids were at home and Dwight had a serious problem with his liver.

Our loving God wanted me to understand clearly that He had our situation in the palm of His mighty hand and we were on His mind at that very second.

From that sacred moment on I understood, in a profound way, just how important our **Memorial Box** stories are to us. God used the little tiny trinkets to reassure me, in the most dramatic way possible, of His ever-present faithfulness, His lavish love and His compassionate care for each of us.

With each concerning situation, I have now learned to turn intentionally (even if only in my mind) directly to our **Memorial Box** and whisper something like this to the Lord, "There are your reminders. Every single one of them is you. Each represents how you have miraculously worked. You have provided. You have rescued when no one thought it was possible. You healed when no one gave hope. You spared her life when every single odd was against her. You provided every single penny we needed. You protected when it looked impossible. You surprised us with such-n-such. And you are here now. You've never left us. And you have this. We are not alone. You will not desert us now."

Over the years, since that moment in Iowa City, as I meet people struggling with life, questioning where God is in the midst of their circumstance and wondering if He even cares, I share with them my Iowa City story. I urge them to begin a **Memorial Box** of their own! I encourage

12

them that God has been faithful to them, even if they can't remember it and He will not fail them now.

Some seasons it is difficult to see God at work, yet, He is present and He is working even when it may not feel like it. The truth is that feelings wane moment by moment. Yet when our life is committed to Christ, He has our back and there is not a situation that we will ever encounter that He has not already gone before us. Our **Memorial Box** serves to remind us in a very concrete way of His constant care for us time after time after time.

Chapter 2

We Will Remember

We actually began our **Memorial Box** over 20 years ago when we realized that we needed a tangible way to remember every single thing that our mighty God has done for us. We know us and we can be so forgetful! So instead of forgetting, each time someone in our family or our family as a whole experience God's protection, His provision, His rescue, His healing or His unexpected blessing we find something that symbolizes what God did. Then we take the object and place it in our **Memorial Box** - a large wooden box with a screen door that rests in our family room.

The Old Testament book of Joshua contains one of the first mentions of having a tangible memorial with the historical account of God's miraculous parting of the Jordan River.

The Bible recounts the story. God's chosen people, the Israelites, had been promised a land flowing with milk and honey when Abraham was their leader. Years later, under the leadership of Moses, they were going to enter the Promise Land, however, the men who were sent in to see the land, were overcome with fear, doubt and unbelief. They chose fear over faith and the entire nation was then forced to wander a full 40 years as a result of their fear. Finally, after 40 years of wandering, under the new leadership of Joshua, it was time to enter the Promise Land, which had actually been promised nearly 500 years before.

The Promise Land was just beyond the Jordan River, and finally! It was time! Forty years of wandering in the desert and now they would be allowed to enter – something their fathers had only dreamed of. But as they stood looking out toward the Promise Land, there was only one thing that stood between them - the Jordan River that was swollen to flood-level.

We can only imagine what the Israelites were thinking as they stood looking at the swollen Jordan River, knowing that God's promise was just on the other side of it and remembering that the previous generation's doubt had kept them from entering it.

The day before they were to enter Joshua told them, "Consecrate yourself, for tomorrow God will do wonders among us." When Joshua told them to consecrate themselves he also gave them a promise: "Tomorrow God is going to do wonders among us." In other words, don't look at the circumstances of the flood-level Jordan River - just get yourself prepared spiritually and watch what God does!

Personally speaking, it is nearly impossible for me to see God working or remember what He has done when I am all wrapped up in worry, fear and doubt. In fact, in some difficult situations, the best thing I can do is to fast. Fasting prepares me spiritually and puts my heart in order to trust my powerful God.

Isn't it also interesting that when God gives a promise, there is often a "flood-level river" between that promise and us? We know that the promise is from the Lord, but in order to get to that promise there is unchartered, even potentially terrifying waters that must be passed through!

God had told Joshua exactly what to do when the day to enter came. The priests carrying the Ark of the Covenant (which represented God's presence) were to go ahead of the Israelites and as the first priest's foot touched the water, the flood-level waters instantly parted! The priests then took the Ark of the Covenant and stood in the middle of the Jordan while the entire nation passed. Only God could get the credit for the water parting and the land in the river bed being completely dry! He had done the humanly impossible! The entire Israelite nation crossed the Jordan River on perfectly dry ground!

Then God gave Joshua some very specific instructions: After the last person has crossed, gather twelve men - one from each of the twelve tribes of Israel. Have the twelve men go back into the middle of the dry Jordan River, to exactly where the priests' feet have been standing holding the Ark of the Covenant. They were each then to gather a rock from that very sacred spot and bring it out of the river and place all twelve together to remember exactly what God had just done!

God told Joshua that the stones would be *"a sign among you"* for the rest of their lives. When their children asked what the stones meant, they were to tell them the story of how God had been with them as He parted and held back the flood-level water for each of the Israelites to pass through on perfectly dry ground!! They were told to *tell their children and their children's children*. Remind them what God has done!

After they had gathered the stones, the Ark of the Covenant, which had been waiting in the middle of the dry Jordan was now moved to the edge of the Jordan

18

and carefully lifted out. When the foot of the last priest was lifted off the dry Jordan, the water rushed to flood level again. The twelve rocks that the men had gathered, would now be a *memorial forever!*

The book of Joshua tells us this: *And those twelve stones, which they took out of the Jordan, Joshua set up at Gilgal. And he said to the people of Israel, "When your children ask their fathers in times to come, 'What do these stones mean?' then you shall let your children know, 'Israel passed over this Jordan on dry ground.' For the LORD your God dried up the waters of the Jordan for you until you passed over, as the LORD your God did to the Red Sea, which he dried up for us until we passed over, so that all the peoples of the earth may know that the hand of the LORD is mighty, that you may fear the LORD your God forever." Joshua 4: 20-24 ESV*

God wanted the Israelites to *tell the story* of His powerful provision so that anyone who heard it would know that the Lord is mighty! God wanted the stones to serve as a reminder for the future. When fear, panic and terror threatened to overtake their hearts they could look at the tangible *memorial* of stones and remember *exactly* what God had done for them.

God told them, "Remind yourselves and your children and your children's children what I have done!"

And that's precisely why our family has a **Memorial**

19

Box. It is our intentional reminder of all that God has done in our family.

Our **Memorial Box** is displayed in our family room and it is filled with all kinds of items that we have gathered over many, many years. Each item is a symbol of God's direct work in our lives: His provision, His protection, His healing or an enormous surprise from His hand! It is so easy to forget what God has done!! But our **Memorial Box** is our very tangible way of remembering just how mighty our God is!!

Over the years, I have given **Memorial Boxes** as wedding gifts, birthday gifts and "just because" gifts to friends. I urge teens, singles, marrieds and empty nesters to begin a **Memorial Box**. My prayerful intention while writing **The Memorial Box** is that God will stir people's hearts to begin to fill their own **Memorial Box** as lasting reminders for future generations!

Truthfully, we actually need to hear each other's stories. We need to be reminded just how powerful our God is. Each story builds our trust, strengthens our faith and encourages hope! Our God can do anything!! *ANYTHING!* He is all-powerful, all knowing and He moves in the most spectacular ways!!

Often our children will ask, "Can I pick something out of the **Memorial Box** for you to tell us the story?" Some of the stories involve them, some are from many years ago, but all are equally captivating.

While looking over the items in our **Memorial Box** we have realized that there is one common thread - when God orchestrates the story, He doesn't do anything ho-hum. Never! He weaves the miraculous through each part of each story, so that in the end, the only glory in each story is all His!! No one can take any credit, because He has done things with breathtaking splendor – so much so that we are left in complete awe because His move was so spectacular! He is so incredible, so breathtaking and the only one worthy of all the praise! In fact He loves each of us so very much that He specializes in surprising us with the miraculous – it's who He is!!

Who could have guessed that a simple wooden box, in our family room, filled with seemingly insignificant items to most, would be used by God to speak in such a powerful way that day in Iowa City?

So it is with great joy and our most humble privilege to share a few of our own personal **Memorial Box** stories.

Our sincere prayer is that each story will encourage hearts, uplift souls, strengthen the faith of all and challenge everyone to begin their own **Memorial Box**!

Chapter 3

The 8th Floor

*"For what you have done I will always praise you
in the presence of your faithful people.
And I will hope in your name, for your name is good."*
Psalm 52:9

This story is one of the most beautiful stories in
our **Memorial Box**. It confirms that our great and
mighty God cares about every little thing we care about
and moves in dramatic ways on our behalf!

It was March 2012 and Dwight and Emma were
in Africa leading a mission team. Our youngest at the
time, Ruby, had only been home for about four months.
Because of her fragile life we were co-sleeping each
night. About 4am I awoke to her rhythmically banging

into my back. Turning over toward her I realized that she was having a grand mal seizure!

Phoning 911 as I ran to Graham's room to wake him, and running back to our room I found Ruby still seizing. In the meantime Graham had gone outside to await the first responders. Ruby was still seizing when they arrived and they quickly administered a rescue med. She continued seizing. The seizure lasted a full 30 minutes – which is horribly long for a seizure! We have since been told that her seizures are life threatening.

When the EMTs and paramedics got her ready to transport to the hospital, I threw my clothes on, grabbed my computer and purse while following behind the stretcher to the waiting ambulance. My mind was going ninety miles an hour and I never thought to bring her diaper bag or even a change of clothes for Ruby or myself. After arriving at the hospital, they put a tiny hospital gown on her and I wadded up the tee shirt she was wearing and threw it in my purse since it was soaked from the seizure.

A few days later when she was ready to be discharged, I realized I had not brought clothes for her to wear home except the tee shirt and when I went to my purse I found it still damp. Since Graham, who was 16 at the time, was already on his way to pick us up, I left him a message.

A few minutes later Graham phoned me and I explained that I really needed him to find a store and run in and buy an outfit for Ruby to wear home. I asked, "Do you think you could find a store?" His response, "Mom, I pulled over in a Wal-Mart to call you!" Wow Lord, You are so amazing! So Graham ran in and found a darling little spring dress for his little *Rubylicious* (as he called her).

When Graham arrived at the hospital I asked him if it was cold outside. "Yes, it's pretty cold, for Phoenix anyway!" It was then that I realized that I did not have any booties or socks for her little teeny-tiny feet.

Since I confide in the Lord about everything, I whispered, "Oh, Lord. What can I put on her feet? It's cold out." I didn't even have a little receiving blanket to wrap them in!

Preparing to discharge, there was a steady stream of medical staff coming in and out of her room. In the back of my mind, again, I whispered to Him, "What about Ruby's feet? What should I do?"

Moments before we were leaving, there was a knock on Ruby's hospital room door. Opening the door, we found a group of smiling young women, probably almost a dozen or so, pulling two wagons. What were the two wagons carrying? They were completely *overflowing* with booties, little girl slippers

24

and adult slippers! They asked, "We are here from Kohl's Department store, could you use any slippers?" Seriously, I almost fell over. I am laughing as I type. Can you believe that? Less than 30 minutes had passed since I had first whispered my need to the Lord! I giggled as I told them that I had just been praying for something to put on my baby girl's feet since it was so cold!

They smiled from ear to ear as they searched their wagons for the teeny-tiniest booties they could find. There they were - princess crowns, no less!! Of course, they fit absolutely perfectly on our tiny African Princess's feet! I mean, why wouldn't they? The entire story was completely miraculous, orchestrated only by God!

If that wasn't miraculous enough of the Lord, after they found Ruby her little Princess slippers, they turned and asked if I would like a pair of slippers. Little did they know that mine were at home in desperate need of replacing! They then handed me a soft pink pair for myself. My bathrobe was pink at the time, making for an extra lavish love gift from the Lord. Truly, He does "above and beyond all we can think or ask!" (Ephesians 3: 20,21)

Of course in the midst of the conversation with the sweet group of volunteers I invited them all in to Ruby's room to show them her "before" picture and then introduce them to our sleeping princess! Hearts seemed to be genuinely touched as I shared with them about our loving God's deep concern for the orphan.

As I went back to wait for the final word that we could go, I sat stunned and giggling. Little would I have guessed, that our faithful God had perhaps days or weeks or even months before been working behind the scenes on Ruby's behalf for that very moment. He had miraculously prompted folks from Kohl's to load wagons for Phoenix Children's on March 2ⁿᵈ, 2012 to walk the 8th floor, bringing Ruby a pair of princess booties to wear home on a chilly Phoenix day!

Can we even begin to grasp all the steps that God orchestrated for that to happen at precisely the perfect moment?

Dear friends, that was not a coincidence! Not a chance! It was all compliments of our ever-faithful God who even cares about one baby girl's feet being warm for the trip home from the hospital. Her princess booties were on the way, before I barely whispered my prayer to my faithful Father, because He is our miracle-working, mountain-moving, awe-inspiring, gasp-giving God!

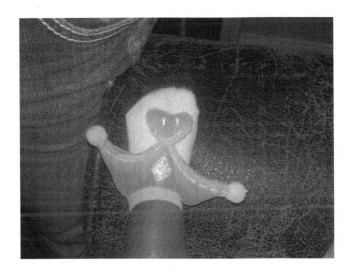

When Ruby outgrew the booties, we placed them in our Memorial Box. They will always remind us that God provides in the most incredible ways if we just ask Him!

"But my God shall supply every need of yours according to His riches in glory in Christ Jesus."
Philippians 4:19

Chapter 4

Captain Smith

It's sometimes hard to comprehend that God truly does care about the little things in our lives. He is never too busy for *anything* that is a thought of ours.

When we think that God is too busy working on the "big stuff" to care about the "little stuff" we are vastly underestimating God's direct involvement in each of our lives! If we think that God doesn't really care unless the situation is enormous, we fail to recognize just how personal God really is and that His deepest desire is for a daily personal relationship with each one of us.

God loves us deeply and desires that we talk to Him about anything that is on our hearts!! He wants us to share with Him all of our concerns, each of our cares, our deepest desires and all of our needs. The Bible confirms over and over throughout scripture, from the first page to the last page, just how much God longs for relationship with us!

As a little girl I heard about Jesus and how much He loved me. I can remember crying when I realized how broken my life was and how much I needed this God who loved me enough to send His only son to die for me. I wanted Him to take away my sin and make me clean! From that day on I purposed to please God and love Him with all my heart.

Somewhere in my early years I was given a Bible and I would spend time reading it each day. While memorizing and meditating on the verses I also decided I was going to obey what it said.

Due to our family dynamics, I spent most of my time in my room, because it was actually the safest place to be. Because of the circumstances I was very lonely and so I talked to Jesus, literally, all day and much of each night. I would tell Him that I was so thankful that He was my friend and I would ask Him to give me the courage to live my life in a way that would only please Him.

I would whisper to Him about everything that I thought of. I remember very vividly, when I was about 9 or 10-years-old, in the midst of my normal talking to Him, I told Him a joke. I laughed with the punch line and imagined that He was laughing too. That might sound silly to some, but He had become my one and only very best friend and I thought He might find that joke funny as well. Looking back on that day I am quite confident that my sweet ever-present Savior was enjoying the innocent little girl I was.

Anyway, since He was my best friend and I had only Him to lean on, I learned to truly talk to Him about everything. There was nothing that I left out. If I thought it, I talked to Him about it.

Before long, I began to realize that He was listening to me and He was moving on my behalf. The stories I could share of those painful days will someday be told, Lord willing, in a book about my life. But for now, let's just say, He was faithful - always forever faithful. In fact, "faithful" has been my most favorite word to describe Him. I tell Him multiple times each day how grateful I am that He is faithful.

By God's grace I was able to publish my first book, **Rescuing Ruby**, in 2015. **Rescuing Ruby** shares the dramatic story of our little Ruby who was found by our fourth oldest, Emma, dying and emaciated in the corner of an orphanage. When Emma found her, Ruby weighed only six pounds and she was over a year old! The way God orchestrated Ruby's rescue is an incredible testimony to His deep love for the orphan, His faithful healing power and His ever-present involvement in our

30

day-to-day lives!

Every now and then I will ask people what their favorite chapter of **Rescuing Ruby** was. Hands down each one responds that their favorite chapter is the one about the British Air pilot! God did miraculous things through one man who knew nothing about Ruby, nothing about her desperate medical situation nor did he know that time was of the essence to get our dying Ruby home!

For those who have read **Rescuing Ruby** you will have extra joy in the following story, which took place in the fall of 2016. It is a testimony to the beautiful power of our great and loving God!! He moves on our behalf even for things that have seemingly little importance to many! *All we have to do is ask Him!*

So backing up a bit, in November of 2011, Emma and I were heading home with broken Ruby in our arms. As we touched down in London, I knew that it was only by God's incredible grace that Ruby had made it safely! In the flurry of collecting all of our bags, tenderly carrying Ruby and making sure we knew where we were going, I had not been able to properly thank the heroic pilot Captain Graham Smith! After the flight he was nowhere to be seen.

I felt bummed when the dust settled knowing that I had not really properly thanked him! Captain Smith had

31

played an enormous role in the rescue of Ruby and he didn't even know how truly significant his part had been.

So while writing **Rescuing Ruby**, I included Captain Smith in the "Dedications". I longed for him to know what exactly his part in her rescue had meant to our family. About that time I began to pray earnestly that God would allow me, one day, to again see Captain Smith and thank him personally.

In my effort to find him I searched for him on LinkedIn, which turned up nothing. Facebook was the same. I even searched on a British Air site, but for all my attempts I found a big nothing. So I kept praying.

Each flight in and out of Africa from 2011 on, I would listen closely to hear the pilot's name as it was announced over the plane's intercom. Surely, the odds of getting him as our pilot for a second time was next to nothing except for the Lord hearing my prayer to have the privilege of thanking him in person!!

In the fall of 2016 I read that British Air would no longer be serving the region of Africa where our Emma is a full-time missionary and I was really distraught. How in the world would I ever be able to thank Captain Smith? Not to mention that they are an amazing airline. But I prayed that God would still make a way!

In the fall of 2016 Liberty and I headed to Africa to visit Emmy, Josh, their son and all her Gems. It had been a full five years since God had orchestrated Captain Smith's instrumental role in piloting Ruby's dramatic rescue out of Africa.

Of course, knowing it would be our last travel on a British Air flight to this region of Africa, I was again asking the Lord to please allow me to run across Captain Smith! As only the Lord would have it, while on the layover in London, I noticed a man waiting near the flight to Africa that seemed to look quite a bit like what I remembered Captain Smith looking like.

"Weird," I thought, "That man almost looks like him." But, of course, it had been five years and the man was not in "Captain" clothes. He was merely someone on the flight wearing civilian clothes. I smiled to myself. I probably had Find-Captain-Smith-Fever or something! Turning my attention elsewhere, I forgot all about the man I had noticed.

Liberty and I were soon able to board and settle in for the ten-hour flight from London to Africa. I listened closely to the flight deck announcement and the names of the crew. But to no avail, Captain Smith was not piloting the flight. Oh well. After some much-needed sleep, we reached our destination in Africa. Going into the terminal, we were able to get our VISAs and head to the luggage carousel.

Scanning the crowd as we waited for the carousel to
begin distributing the luggage, I turned and spotted the
same man, this time he was on the far side waiting for
his luggage. He was talking to a gentleman and the
more I stared at him the more I wondered if this could be
him? His smile looked the same and his countenance had
such a kind appearance!

Calling over my shoulder to Liberty, "Follow me!"
as I bee-lined toward the man. Once close enough to
overhear them talking, but not looking at them directly (I
couldn't be too obvious – ha!) another man appeared
beside the two and questioned, "Are you Captain
Smith?" I glanced waiting for his answer and sure
enough he smiled and responded, "Yes!"

Oh my gracious! God - You are incredible! Here he
was, less than six feet from me! I was trying to hide my
giddiness and be patient as he finished up talking to the
two gentlemen!

After five years of waiting, almost to the very day,
what are the odds that the last flight I would take into
Africa on British Air would also be carrying Captain
Smith as a passenger? Zero - but for our most faithful,
miraculous God!!

As the two men he had been talking with gathered
their luggage to walk away, I turned toward him and

questioned as casually as possible, "Captain Smith?" (Yeah, I know, in my over-moon-giddiness I was trying so hard to be casual, but I know I was beaming from ear to ear!) I was beyond excited - like jump-up-and-down-shrieking-excited! I mean, seriously! What were the odds humanly speaking?

Captain Smith smiled and nodded as I proceeded to refresh his memory of the desperate situation five years earlier. He remembered it, questioning, "Your daughter had serious medical needs, didn't she?" I confirmed that that was our baby girl!

As we talked, I pulled out a 'before' and 'after' picture of our miracle girl and showed him. He seemed so pleased! I then unzipped the front pouch of my carry-on and pulled out a copy of my book, Rescuing Ruby, that I had *already* personally written in for him before leaving the house. (I guess that was my faith-in-action!) Before handing it to him, I asked if he would read it and he enthusiastically replied, "Yes!" I told him that he was also mentioned in the Dedications.

I asked if I could hug him. He smiled and said I could. I hugged that miracle pilot and thanked him for his part in rescuing our Ruby!

Since Liberty was with me, I questioned if it would be okay for her to take our picture. He smiled and agreed!

Obviously friends, there is no doubt that our almighty God had orchestrated that meeting! If Captain Smith had been the pilot on the flight that day I might not have seen him to talk to him. But God had something better – just like He always does! Captain Smith was riding on the same flight and at the luggage carousel where I could easily talk to him, hand him the book and give him a giant hug!

Don't ever think that any concern of yours is not a concern to the Lord. He longs for us to talk to Him and He continuously loves to move on our behalf!

In our Memorial Box is the picture of Captain Smith and I. We will tell our children and our children's children the story to remind them that nothing is too small nor is anything too difficult for our great God!

I will sing of the loving kindness of the LORD forever;
To all generations I will make known
Your faithfulness with my mouth.
Psalm 89:1

Chapter 5

BOOM!

Everyone will have monumental events or seasons. Many events will have been planned, dreamed about, highly anticipated and definitely worked toward - like a wedding, a cross-country move, maybe an addition to the family or even a job change. These hoped-for changes will produce great joy as lives are changed forever!

Yet as wonderful as some events can be, there are other significant occurrences that were not planned, nor were they anticipated and definitely would never have been hoped for. Instead each of these situations left trauma, grief and heartache as all the lives touched by them would also be changed forever.

It is paramount for us to see God at work in our painful, traumatic, and devastating seasons. In fact, the

Bible speaks of God's presence during times of trauma. Two verses I've turned to often: Psalm 46:1 *"He is our refuge and strength, a very present help in trouble"* and *"The Lord is close to the brokenhearted and saves those who are crushed in spirit."* Psalm 34:18

The assurance of His faithful presence provides peace during the unexpected seasons, hope in our sorrows and comfort in our losses. Each time we find ourselves in the midst of a painful circumstance; we choose to remember what God has done in the past, which gives us bold confidence that He is at work, no matter what. He has never failed us. Not once.

One of the items in our Memorial Box is a small log home, which serves to remind our family of the supernatural, miracle-working faithfulness of our Almighty God through one of the most painful seasons in our lives. It was one of our family's most significant events and would forever change how we viewed life.

****

As far back as I can remember my mom spoke often about the three life-threatening fires she had experienced when she was young. One of the fires she was in, she jumped safely into the arms of a stranger who happened to be passing by. After the third fire, she learned that her father had set each of their three homes on fire in an effort to collect insurance money. Clearly my grandfather was a cold, calculating, and hate-filled man.

Because of the trauma she had endured, my mom talked regularly with us about fire safety. Growing up I became very fire conscious as well. Almost every single night of my life, to this day, I walk through the house to make sure that escape routes are clear. I think about items, no matter how small, being in front of doors at night.

And I would buy smoke alarms to hand out to anyone who didn't have one: friends, missionaries overseas, our children's friends, and orphanages in countries we've served. Really I've been a smoke alarm nut.

Of course, I prayed many times, *"Lord, please don't let our home ever have a fire."*

In 2004 we moved to Colorado to pastor. After being there for a couple of years, we bought a little tiny 30-year-old log home set on three acres in the countryside. It was perfect for our family. The little log home reminded us of a cottage my precious father-in-love had built once-upon-a-time that held lots of beautiful memories for our family!

As we moved into our log home, we had a security system installed because of a man who had been stalking me and had entered our home. Although I had a

Permanent Protective Order, we knew it would be wise to have a security system as well.

When the gentleman was installing the security system he asked if we also wanted a smoke alarm hooked in. Yes! Absolutely! I reasoned that it would be a "back-up" since we already had several other smoke alarms.

In November 2008, while in California for Thanksgiving with our daughter, Abigail and her husband Ryan, we received a phone call from the alarm company that there was an error registering for the smoke alarm part of our system. They called several times and eventually we asked our neighbor if he would go and unhook it.

We returned from Thanksgiving and three days later two of our teens, Graham and Emma, left with me for Africa to bring home our little Elizabeth and Elijah. We didn't even think about the smoke alarm being unhooked - after all we had several other battery operated ones.

Emma, Graham, and I returned from Africa on December 18th, 2008 with two new babies! Soon it was Christmas and New Years and somewhere in there I had a dream. I woke up with a start having dreamed that our little log home had burned down. A week or so later, I again dreamed that we had lost our home to a fire. Once awake, I felt such an urgency that we needed to get that smoke alarm system fixed, re-hooked up and ready to go.

Things around the house were wild with the new babies, our oldest son was home before deploying, and Dwight was about to leave for his annual prayer retreat. The day before Dwight was to leave I asked him if he could please call the young man, Kyle, who had installed the alarm system and have him return to fix it. Dwight phoned him early Monday morning and Kyle agreed to come Tuesday morning to fix it. Dwight left Monday afternoon for his retreat and our son also left to go back to his base.

By lunch on Tuesday, January 13, 2009 Kyle had finished fixing the smoke alarm in our security system. That afternoon I began to feel a strange uneasiness. It was out of character for me and I wondered why I was suddenly feeling so unsettled.

That afternoon I also began to notice an odd smell. It wasn't something burning at all but it almost smelled like rolls baking in an oven. I walked around the house to see if I could figure out what was producing the smell. I couldn't put my finger on it but it almost seemed to be coming from the laundry room.

Given the weird uneasiness, in hindsight, I wished I had gone up to our bedroom, closed the door and asked the Lord to tell me what the uneasiness was coming from. Was He warning me of something? It was a not a good feeling I was having and yet, I didn't stop to ask. And what was the smell? In my humanness, I just didn't put the smell and uneasiness together.

Later that afternoon the little ones and I had to take Emma and Graham in to town to worship practice. That evening, while pulling down the long lane to our home, I actually said to the kids, "I think I should turn the van around in case we have to leave in a hurry, you know, like if we have an emergency." I had never said anything like that before, but I turned our big van around and parked.

Soon after heading into our home, I began getting the babies ready for bed. After reading to them, rocking them and putting them in their cribs, I went to tuck Liberty and Isaiah in. With the four youngest in bed, I came into the kitchen and commented to Emma, "I don't know what it is honey, but I feel so uneasy." I can't remember that I have ever said that before either. Eventually Graham, Emma and I went to bed right around midnight.

I fell asleep quickly but before long I began to hear a steady beeping. I had a hard time waking, since I hadn't been asleep long, and was actually trying to incorporate the beeping into my dream. In my very sleepy state I eventually realized that it was a true beeping in the house and not part of a dream! I sleepily went downstairs to see what it was. It was about 1:30 am. It turned out to be the alarm system's lone smoke alarm that Kyle had fixed just hours before!

I kind of looked around, still more asleep than awake but it had quit beeping not long after I got downstairs. As I climbed back up the stairs I decided it must just be a faulty smoke alarm and I would call Kyle to replace it in the morning.

Two hours later, at 3:30am, I woke up to the smoke alarm beeping and went downstairs again. I was still so groggy but I noticed that "rolls in the oven" smell seemed stronger. Since our bedroom was the only one upstairs and the kids were all asleep in the three little bedrooms below I glanced in their rooms. The smoke alarm had again stopped beeping not long after I came down the stairs.

I sleepily climbed back up the stairs and crawled into bed. I was back to sleep in no time.

At about 5:30 I was awakened for the third time to the smoke alarm beeping. Pulling my bathrobe on, I went downstairs again. I prefer to be up early to spend time with the Lord when the house is quiet, yet I was really tired and couldn't decide if I should try to get a little more sleep after checking things out downstairs.

44

But this time the smoke alarm did not stop beeping. I wandered around the house trying to see if there was something I was missing. I also wondered if I smelled smoke this time? It almost seemed like it was coming from the laundry room. I went down and looked but could not see anything. Then the beeping again stopped.

In hindsight, yes, I should have called the fire department right then. But remember we had multiple ceiling smoke alarms independent from the one Kyle had just fixed the day before. Not one of the independent smoke alarms beeped even once and that didn't make sense except for the fact that this newly "fixed" smoke alarm must really not be fixed after all. The alarm company did not call at any point to see if it was a true alarm or a false alarm which made me believe that it was just the alarm that was faulty so it was must not be registering in their system.

Our little log house had hot water baseboard heat but we were primarily heating with wood in our wood stove. The fire in the stove had gone out hours before so once I decided to stay up, I went to build a fire. Within minutes the alarm started going off again. I looked at the clock. It was about 6:15am. I tried to think of someone I could call to come and help me figure out if there was a true problem. I thought of our close friends, Terry and Tavvy, who lived not far, but I hated to wake them.

Within a minute or two it was really going off. I went back to the laundry room and got down on my knees next to the box that heats the water for the baseboard. It is an old box, but as I was getting down on my knees to look under it, I distinctly recalled the home inspector tapping it during our home inspection and saying, "This thing will last forever. It's old, but they never give out." So as I looked under the box (it was raised off the floor a couple of inches) I saw that there were two identical tiny trails of smoke inside heading upwards into the box. I thought, "That's weird, I wonder if that is normal?"

I looked at the clock and thought that I would call Dwight at 7am. He is so exhausted and I didn't want to wake him out of a sound sleep. I again tried to think of someone who might be up and could come over to see if they thought those tiny trails of smoke were normal. Should I call Terry?

Oh dear ones reading our story...God was extremely merciful and faithful, BUT learn from my mistakes! Call 911 immediately!

Exactly at 7am I dialed Dwight's cell number. He had been sound asleep. I told him what was going on and in his sleepy stupor he told me to turn some dial off on the hot water baseboard box. I had no clue what he was talking about but still on the phone with him, I went

46

down to our laundry room to look at the hot water baseboard box. I couldn't figure it out and walked out of the laundry room and to the kitchen as we continued talking. Suddenly, the alarm started beeping faster.

With the alarm suddenly beeping faster, I ran (still on the phone) back to the laundry room and this time when I opened the door the laundry room was filled with smoke!! I screamed into the phone, "I have to call 911 the room is filled with smoke!" In my panic, I hung up on him.

I ran for the house phone (which was still in my hand) and ran back to the laundry room. This time as I entered the laundry room I saw the flames! The floor was on fire and the flames were heading up the wall behind the hot water baseboard box!

Dialing 911, the operator answered, "What is the address of your emergency?"

Remembering that we are always to speak slowly, I gave her my address and continued, "My home is on fire! I am home alone. My husband is out of town and I have six children sleeping. I have to wake them!"

Her only response, **"I can't understand you."**

Slowly (or at least to me it was slowly) repeating myself, "MY HOUSE IS ON FIRE! I – AM – HOME – ALONE! MY HUSBAND IS OUT OF TOWN! THERE ARE FLAMES IN MY HOME! I HAVE SIX CHILDREN

SLEEPING! PLEASE HURRY!"

Again she responded, "I cannot understand you. What is your emergency?" My heart was racing as I repeated it yet a third time - enunciating every single word as slowly as I could yet knowing there were now flames, the laundry room floor was on fire and the babies were asleep less than 10 feet from the flames.

It was then that I realized that right next to the flames was the hot water tank. I wondered if a gas hot water tank could blow up? I had no clue, but that thought made me frantic even more!

After repeating myself the third time I could hear her turn to someone near her, "I cannot understand her." At that point I began to get hysterical. Why could she not understand me? I was repeating things slowly and enunciating carefully. Instantly I heard another women's voice and for the fourth time I repeated it all again! She questioned, "Are you trying to report a house fire?"

Again, as slowly as possible I repeated the same thing. "YES! I AM HOME ALONE! MY HUSBAND IS OUT OF TOWN! I HAVE SIX CHILDREN SLEEPING AND I HAVE TO GET THEM OUT!"

She seemed to understand and responded, "Stay on the line." I was now crying and screamed, "I CAN'T – I HAVE TO GET MY BABIES!" I hung up on her.

I ran down the short hallway: Boys door first on the left – Girls door directly across the hall on the right – I was pounding the open doors with my fists and screaming, "Get up, get up, get your coats on!! The house is on fire! Help me get the babies! Get up!! Get up!! Grab some blankets! Get your coats and get the babies out of the house! The house is on fire!"

The bathroom door is next on the right and next on the left was the baby's room. Across from the baby's room was the laundry room. I opened the door of the laundry room and the smoke was choking me. The flames were filling the left side of the room.

I ran back to the phone and called Dwight (although I don't remember this). I screamed, "The house is on fire!" I then hung up on him again. He threw his stuff in the car and drove to the front office building where he was staying. Running inside and tossing the cabin keys on the counter, he yelled, "My home is on fire!" The owners screamed, "GO! Just GO!" Jumping in his car, he sped toward our home.

I could not find my purse. My cell phone was completely dead. I frantically ran around the kitchen/living room trying to think what to do. Emma and Graham were getting Elijah and Elizabeth's coats on.

Liberty, who was nine at the time, stood like a statue at the bottom of the stairs crying hysterically. It was so uncharacteristic of her to be hysterical; she's my laid back one! I took Liberty by the shoulders and looked her straight in the eyes, "You can't get hysterical! You must think! Get your shoes on and get your coat on - NOW!"

The entire time, the ONLY smoke alarm that was blaring was the one that Kyle had fixed less than 24 hours before!!

Seriously, I could not have done it without my big kids. They could think much clearer than me. I couldn't find my purse and I needed my keys so we could start

50

the car for the kids to stay warm. It was nowhere.

Graham appeared with our handheld fire extinguisher. He went with me to the laundry room and on the way we realized the extinguisher wouldn't be enough. Dwight had mentioned flour so I ran to the kitchen for flour. Knowing how rural we were as well as the fact that it was a volunteer fire department, I knew the trucks would take awhile to get to our beloved little log home. I had thought (foolishly) that maybe I could slow the flames. Emma was with me this time as I held the flour bucket and opening the door we saw the room basically engulfed with flames and filled with thick smoke. I closed the door.

I then yelled to Graham, "Do you think I should try to run through the laundry room and open the outside door? I don't want daddy to have to replace the door that the firemen will have to kick in."

I'll never forget my precious Graham's troubled expression. Undoubtedly I was not thinking clearly and in denial. Our home was on fire! Together Graham and I opened the door and the smoke was choking us and the flames filled the room. We closed the door.

Later the firemen, when hearing of my desire to open the outside door told me that had I done that I would have been engulfed in flames the second the outside air hit the fire.

It had been about one degree every morning for several days and realizing I just had a nightgown and bathrobe on, I ran upstairs to our room to try to find a pair of pants. I couldn't find any. I ran back and forth trying to think of a pair of pants I could pull on.

I am an organized person and I knew where my pants were, but being so distraught, I just couldn't think. I believe God wouldn't allow me to recall where they were because we really needed to leave - NOW!

I ran back downstairs to see where the kids were. Little did I know that a moment after I came down from trying to find a pair of pants, Graham, who was 14 at the time, had decided, on his own, to run upstairs to get our family photo albums. However, while up in the loft, the smoke was so bad he was driven back downstairs. God was again so faithful! If Graham had been overcome with smoke, I would have not had a clue where he was!

Emma found my purse - she had put it away while cleaning the night before. Elijah, Elizabeth, Isaiah and Liberty were in the car with the dogs. I ran out onto the porch and dashed over toward the car to see if the four were really in the car.

I ran back to the house and wandered about trying to think but completely paralyzed. What should I grab? Learn from my mistakes – anyone whose home is on fire needs to just leave the house!! Get out! Don't grab anything but your loved ones!

Graham was now on the phone with 911 and I could hear him quietly saying, "No, we are not out of the house yet. Yes, my little siblings are in the car with the dogs. (pause) No my mom, sister and I are still in the house. My mom is trying to think of what else we need to get. (pause) Yes I know, but my mom is still trying to figure out what to get. (pause) No we are still inside the house." He turned to me, "Mom, 911 said we need to leave now." Another few seconds passed and I could hear him repeat again, "No, we are still inside." Turning to me and very matter-of-factly he spoke with such calm, "Mom we need to leave the house."

It was then, because of Graham's firm urgings that I said to Graham and Emma, "Okay, let's go." It was hard to leave. I just wanted to stop it all. I wanted to be able to fix it. I adored our little log home. It was, to this day, the homiest place we have ever lived in. It was tiny and cozy, nestled on three acres with a breathtaking view of the Rockies.

Emma, Graham and I, walked slowly, arms wrapped around each other and huddled together out of our precious little log home, onto the porch, down the sidewalk and into the driveway. Graham was still on the phone with 911. He told the operator, "Yes. We are out of the house." She remained on the phone as we climbed into the car. Literally, and I mean literally, the instant we sat down in the car, we turned our eyes to the house and there was a giant, loud, "BOOM!" while simultaneously thick black smoke poured out from every opening: the crawl space vents, windows, and the roof! It was surreal!

A few days after the fire we were allowed to listen to both my first call and Graham's 911 calls. Our phone was muffled but I was also speaking much faster than I had imagined. In my panicked state, my voice also rose higher than it naturally is and I was difficult to understand. Graham's call was different. He spoke so calmly I was amazed. He has always been our steady, unruffled one. When there is a crisis he is the one I want beside me, as he calmly reassures me that everything will be okay.

As I said, the 911 operator was still on the phone with Graham when we sat down in the car and you can plainly hear in the recording Graham say loudly, "OH CRAP!" before the line went dead. After hearing the recording, we asked Graham what was happening when he said, "OH CRAP!" He responded that that was when we sat down in the car, turned to face the house, heard the loud BOOM and saw the smoke pour out!

We are certain, that had we still been in the house at

that moment, quite possibly it would have been too late to get out - which would have been within a minute of actually leaving the house.

Later the fire expert, who came to inspect our home, told us that it was the worst fire he had seen in many years. He also said that the fire reached over 800 degrees and he also confirmed that if we had stayed in the home "about five minutes more" we would have perished.

Our faithful God had rescued us, in spite of my denial, in spite of my lack of understanding the intensity of it all, in spite of my naiveté. We will never be able to thank God for His faithful mercy over our family that terrifying morning.

As we watched our beloved log home burn I remember sobbing and sobbing. My cherished log home. I had always dreamed of living in one and this was my dream come true. It wasn't fancy, it wasn't big, it wasn't new, but it was snuggly and cozy with it's gabled roof and dormers, exposed logs on the walls, the gorgeous log stair rail, an old wisteria outside the kitchen door, gobs of lilac bushes running along the backside - not to mention that view of the Rockies! Our little log home was like a comfortable friend, always welcoming!

Yes, all temporal things, but nonetheless, familiar to our souls and excruciatingly painful to abruptly lose.

While still waiting for the fire department to arrive, I

remember jumping out of the car and pacing while calling out loudly to the Lord, "Okay Lord, please hurry the fire department! And please would you help me to get this right? I want to honor you through this whole trial. Give me your peace, your wisdom, your words. I want to get this right!"

Before long I called a friend and asked them to put it on my blog asking people to pray. Little did I know that our fire would be used by God to catapult my quiet little blog around the world as sweet friends shared it and soon thousands of readers from around the world were stopping by each day.

The first person on the scene was the sheriff. He was very nice and so concerned that the kids were all out. I assured him that they were in the car, along with the two dogs.

Next, an enormous fire truck arrived! As it started down our long lane, because of the bulging snow banks that lined each side of the narrow lane, it became completely stuck. It would not budge at all! The firefighters had to lay the hoses around the truck and then set up a pool at the side of the road.   The pool was about the size of a long backyard pool. They had to go to the hospital a few miles away to pump water, which they hauled to the pool on the side of the road. Before long 15 fire trucks were lining our little country road.

Dwight was speeding back and had to drive through the National Forest where there is zero cell service most of the ride. As he drove toward home, his denial kicked in. He thought, "It's a little smoke, it will be fine. They will arrive and put it out." But as he came up to the hill to our home, he turned to the left and saw the huge cloud of smoke billowing up into the sky and shouted, "That's our home!" We hugged and cried when he arrived. We were both in shock as we stood and watch the events unfold.

Word traveled fast through our little city and close friends came to comfort us. My dear friend, Carie, took chocolate milk and stuffed animals to each of our kids who were staying at a friend's home across the road. They would soon learn that all their special things were now gone. Carie then came to the house and stood holding my hand, tears dripping beside mine.

We watched as firefighter after firefighter came out of our home took off their mask, red-faced and coughing and spitting junk out. They would then switch tanks and go back in again.

Before Dwight had arrived home, I had asked the Fire Chief if he thought they would save our home. I held my breath. I wanted him to say, "Yes, no problem. Everything is going to be fine." He didn't. *I guess they only do that in movies.*

He said, "I don't know. I am concerned for the safety of my people. I am concerned that they will be trapped in the crawl space. There is a danger that the floors will collapse." (Which they did in part of the house.) I asked him to please just pull his people out. Forget the house!

As our home burned, I phoned Kyle. He answered cheerily, "Hey Linn!" Without any hesitation I burst out crying and through choking sobs I told him, "Kyle! You know how you just came yesterday and fixed our smoke alarm? Our home is burning down at this moment. The smoke alarm you fixed is the only one that worked!! The only one! Do you know if you hadn't come yesterday we would likely all be gone now? Thank you for coming. Thank you so much!"

Someone came to get Emma's horse Daisy to safety. The nearest Christian Radio station was in New Mexico and after hearing they went on the air and asked people to pray and prayer chains were mobilized.

That night I couldn't sleep. My body jerked and jolted. Surely it had been my worst fear realized! I just cried and cried.

The next morning, as I was walking by the sleeping bag Graham was in at our friend's home, he told me that his stomach had been killing him for several hours. Dwight and I questioned where the pain was and

58

realized it was probably appendicitis. I headed to the ER with him and within hours he was in surgery. There were a few complications and he actually had to stay in the hospital two nights.

The second morning in the hospital Dwight called to tell me that Graham's black lab and faithful companion, Lucy, had died the day before. She had been at the vets for surgery the day before the fire and had just stayed there the day of the fire. The vet said she had been doing great, but he had gone in the morning after the fire and found her dead. Three days in a row: Fire, Graham's surgery and the next day finding Graham's dog had died.

Yet through it all, our God was completely faithful. Were parts terrifying? Yes! Was it something we would choose to go through again? Never. But God had been completely faithful.

You know friends, whether on the mountaintops or in the valleys, God is always completely faithful. He never changes. We can count on His character and His faithfulness even when we don't understand the trial we are going through.

The day of the fire and throughout the aftermath, our strength came from remembering all the times He had been faithful in the past. Remembering gave us the confidence that He would be faithful, no matter what the days held. Even on the darkest day, His presence, His goodness, His mercy and His loving kindness were evident. I am reminded of Psalm 59:16, "But as for me, I shall sing of Your strength; Yes, I shall joyfully sing of Your loving kindness in the morning, for You have been my stronghold and a refuge in the day of my distress."

A small log cabin stands in our Memorial Box to remind us of the day God rescued us in a powerful way.

The LORD is my strength and my shield;
My heart trusts in Him, and I am helped;
Therefore my heart exults,
And with my song I shall thank Him.
Psalm 28:7

Chapter 6

The Angel of the Lord

Now being perfectly honest, I battled an intense inner struggle for weeks after the fire. Powerful regrets plagued me. Every bit of my world had been shaken. I struggled most with this: How could I have ignored that uneasy feeling and not gone to the Lord and asked Him about it?

In order to understand why that was so troubling to me, allow me to back up a speck.

One morning just weeks before the fire, while still in Africa bringing the babies home, I was reading my Bible and the Lord led me to a verse I had never noticed before:

> *The LORD confides in* <u>*those who fear Him*</u>*;*
> *He makes his covenant known to them. Psalm 25:14*

I immediately knew that the Lord was speaking to me and so I began to meditate on this verse. I felt like it confirmed many things over my life but it also challenged me. I now understood why the Lord had spoken so many times to me over my life - because I have a very respectful fear of Him and so I strive to please Him each day.

The verse also made me realize that if I continued to respectfully obey (fear) the Lord, He would continue to confide secrets in me. I was so excited and I meditated on this verse over and over in the next few weeks.

Less than four weeks after returning from Africa the fire broke out. Trying to sort through things in my head after the fire, I wondered: In light of Psalm 25:14 – why hadn't the Lord told me that the house was about to catch on fire so we could have averted such a trauma? Or, a better question I wondered was: If I had gone upstairs when I was feeling such uneasiness and knelt beside our bed and been still and waited would He have shown me that the fire was starting to smolder under the house? These thoughts *tormented* me.

Ever been there? Maybe something has happened in your life and you grapple with trying to understand exactly what God is doing? Or perhaps like me, you just aren't sure how you could have missed the warning signs to an event that changed your life?

When my dear friend Celestia came to visit a few weeks later I asked her. She questioned me, "Linn, are you someone who continually lives your life wanting to hear the Lord? (Yes!) If the Lord speaks, do you listen? (Yes!) Do you hear the Lord speak without having to go kneel beside your bed? (Yes!) Well then Linn, if the Lord was going to tell you about the fire beforehand, you did not need to go upstairs and kneel beside your bed. Tears began to fall as she spoke those words.

Yet continued to trouble me and a few weeks later the Lord began to put it all together for me. It was then that our faithful God reassured me that He was in control the entire time. It came through a comment my oldest brother, Dan, left on my blog after I wrote about the fire, Graham's surgery and Graham's dog Lucy. Here's what my brother wrote:

"I was laying in bed early this morning about 4 am my time and I saw in my mind's eye that Satan had come to exchange your beauty for ashes, as we know he comes to steal, kill, and destroy. He tried to start the fire late in the night when no one would awaken, but the Angel of the Lord was there keeping the wood too wet to burn. Satan wanted to take you all, but the Angel of the Lord said, "No, you can have the house, you can have Lucy, and you can take Graham thru the valley of the shadow of death, but NO, you cannot have them."

You are doubly blessed in all this, for you have not only been able to assemble the family God gave you a vision for, but God allowed you to carry them all out of dangers grasp.

This was your Exodus experience; your family has walked right past the grim reaper and survived. This is a time of rejoicing. Of all the outcomes that could have been, this is the one you would have chosen. Julie and I have wept with you and we rejoice with you in life.

Blessings, Your Big Brother

When I read Dan's words I knew it was from the Lord for me. He was right!! When the smoke alarm had gone off at 1:30am I could not even figure out what it was. I had tried to incorporate it into my dream before realizing that it was something outside my sleep realm. I had stumbled downstairs and not really had a clue what was going on. If I had found the floor on fire at that time, humanly speaking, I am not certain that we would not have made it out in time, I was just too out of it and sleepy, barely able to think.

Two hours later, at 3:30am, when the smoke alarm went off again, I barely remember getting up and looking around. Again, I am convinced if the floor had been on fire then, it would have been deadly and disastrous. And no, there is no way on God's green earth that I would have ever left the house without my kids. I would have died trying to get them all out.

Over the next couple of weeks, my brother's words (which I found of great comfort) tumbled around my head as I still wrestled with "God whispers secrets to those who fear Him." It just didn't all make sense to my soul, until one beautiful Sunday morning.

While still living in the hotel and hunting for a rental, Dwight came into our hotel room, as we were getting ready for church. The first thing he said was, "Did you read your Bible yet? (We were both on the Daily Reading Plan at the time.) Linny listen to this:

> *The angel of the LORD encamps around*
> *those who fear him, and he delivers them.*
> *Psalm 34:7"*

The minute Dwight quoted the familiar verse I started to sob. Tears plunking away and right at that instant, the Lord brought it all together for me.

Because I fear the Lord, our protective God had had the Angel of the Lord there the night of the fire. Yes, the Angel of the Lord had been keeping the wood wet until I was awake and able to get the kids out. The Angel of the Lord had delivered the kids and I. From that moment on I felt an instant peace about that aspect of the fire.

I believe the Lord allowed the fire for a reason

although we will never know exactly why. I believe that He *"will cause all things to work together for good to those who love Him and are called according to His purpose."* (Romans 8:28)

I believe if He had wanted me to know we were about to have a fire He would have told me. And yes, I believe He had the angel of the Lord keep the wood wet till I was awake enough to get the kids up and out. I am convinced (now!) that the *literal* Angel of the Lord was there the entire night, watching, keeping the wood wet, protecting, faithfully ministering to the kids and I....

Although there were many aspects of the fire and the aftermath that were painfully hard, the Lord did bring many beautiful things out of it.

I have peace about it all, every single aspect. Would I do things differently if our home were on fire? **YES!** Absolutely! I would grab the kids and run. That's it. I would call 911 once we were all safe outside.

Yet through it all, the Lord was completely faithful each painful step of the way! **Regardless of all the loss, all the adjustments, the many nightmares, the months of rebuilding another home, the years of insurance to deal with... the entire time, our merciful Lord was our comfort, our strength and our ever-faithful friend.**

In our Memorial Box we have a picture of an angel, ripped and powerful...to symbolize the *mighty* Angel of the Lord who was present and protected us that bitter winter night.

But as for me, I shall sing of Your strength;
Yes, I shall joyfully sing of Your loving kindness
in the morning,
For You have been my stronghold
And a refuge in the day of my distress.
Psalm 59:16

Chapter 7

He Moved Them

After the fire we grieved for all the photos, family videos, and precious memoires we had gathered over 30+ years married. There are things and then there are *things*. Some things are easy to let go of while others just hurt to let go of.

When preparing to bring Elijah and Elizabeth home, we had decorated their room with old quilts, teddy bears and a few heirlooms from family. Although they were only home less than four weeks before the fire, I had loved rocking the babies and admiring the beautiful old family treasures tucked against the old log walls.

One of our treasures was an old quilt box. My mom is a beautiful, gifted artist who had painted a scene of a group of Amish women quilting on the front of the old quilt box. There were two little Amish children peeking out from under the table while the Amish women quilted together. It was stunning!! I loved staring at that picture my mom had painted as my babies rocked in my arms.

Many years earlier, while visiting Dwight's parents, his dad had pulled Dwight and I aside to come upstairs to his little study in their home. Slowly he had pulled out a little white box that had been hidden behind some books on the shelves. Opening the box he lifted out an incredibly old pair of baby shoes. When we saw them our mouths dropped open – they were amazing! Dwight's dad explained that they had been in the family for generations and he really wanted us to have them. He, himself, had worn them as a baby. They had been meticulously crafted by hand and on the underside of the shoes it was written: 1757

We were unaware that the shoes even existed!! We humbly received the precious gift and tucked them in our luggage for our ride back to Virginia where we were pastoring. Months later we were heading out of town and remembered the little shoes. Where should we hide them? We ended up putting them in the bottom of the old quilt box my mom had painted for us. Years passed and every now and then we would pull out the little shoes and admire their beauty and talk about all the people in the Saunders lineage who might have worn them.

After the fire Dwight, the kids and I cried and cried for all that we had lost. Grieving is real after a fire. And almost immediately Dwight and I both thought of the shoes. They had been in the bottom of the quilt box, which had been in Elijah and Elizabeth's room.

Since the fire had started in the crawlspace under the laundry room and had quickly spread to Elijah and Elizabeth's room, everything in it was destroyed basically beyond recognition.

One of the baby's cribs

Yet we hoped beyond hope and both ran to find the quilt box, which now sat on the front lawn, charred and completely destroyed. Realizing the little heirloom shoes had been in the very bottom, we knew there was really no hope – *unless GOD!!*

As soon as I saw how destroyed that quilt box was I began to sob and pray. The God of the Universe had done so many things for us that I knew that He could still have protected the shoes!

The shoes were certainly not something that is too difficult for Him! In fact scripture tells us in Jeremiah 32:27 *"Nothing* is too difficult for Him!" At that moment I said aloud while bawling, "This is not too difficult for you God. You can put those shoes under a snow bank for us to find in the spring! You can do it anyway you want to. You can resurrect them. You can do anything – just help us to find those shoes!!"

Now if the average person looked at all the charred-beyond-recognition-items they would have laughed at that prayer. It looked impossible!! But we stood knowing that God loves to do what man deems impossible.

We told our dear friends who came to help us sift through the ashes, "If you should happen upon an old antique pair of baby shoes or even a piece of something that looks like old shoes – please do NOT throw it out – call us immediately. Sift carefully and cautiously – we know those shoes are out there somewhere!" A week passed and there was no sign of the shoes. We kept praying.

I specifically kept asking the Lord to put them in the snow bank, reminding Him what a shock and glorious surprise it would be to find in the spring. We kept looking. Then on Saturday, January 24, 2009, a full 10 days after the fire, I was up in our room cataloging. There were some precious friends helping. Carie, Irma, Beth and others were graciously wearing masks and going through items and listening to my stories of things that were once treasures.

Many others were helping Dwight. Emma and Graham each had a couple of their friends helping them. Everyone was helping us catalog and carry the items to the dumpster.

Upstairs in our bedroom my friends had pulled stuff out of the little cubby we had off our master bathroom. Our master bathroom was bite sized and this little cubby was used for seasonal clothes. The laundry room was directly below the cubby and yet miraculously the cubby floor had not been destroyed.

They had pulled everything out and lined it up so I could go through piece by piece and see if there was anything that I just couldn't bear to part with. Everything had been ruined by the black smoke, soot and heavy water damage, yet as I moved through the items, I came across a little box. I remember looking at

72

the box in bewilderment, because my traumatized brain was trying to recognize. *This box meant something,* yet my brain couldn't quite remember. I will never forget my memory tugging to recall the familiar box…it was the weirdest feeling. Puzzled, seconds of attempting to retrieve the memory as I slowly opened the box and found inside a tiny little antique knobby glass. Still trying to recall, I lifted the glass out and the tissue paper underneath it and began to scream wildly!! **There were our 1757 heirloom shoes!!**

I was now shouting in utter hysteria as I jumped up and over boxes and clothes and piles of smoky, soot-covered stuff! Making my way out of our room and into the loft, at the top of my lungs, "Whitey!! Whitey!! The shoes!! The shoes!! We have the shoes!!"

People came from everywhere. Some honestly thought someone had died I was screaming so hysterically! At one point I remember turning to my precious friend, Carie, and seeing tears streaming down her face as she had also been begging God for the shoes to reappear!!

Our miraculous God had moved the shoes from that little quilt box to the cubby. *They **had been** in the quilt box — there is NO doubt!* I am confident that the night before the fire – while the Angel of the Lord was keeping the wood wet, He had gone and taken the precious shoes and put them in the cubby. No one will ever be able to convince me otherwise! He gets all the glory!!

Friends, maybe you have a situation that looks utterly impossible. We pray our story, encourages you that our God *can do anything*. He is not limited because of a fire that burns at over 800 degrees, He is not limited to where something was and He is never limited at all by any circumstances. He is willing to do the miraculous for you as well!

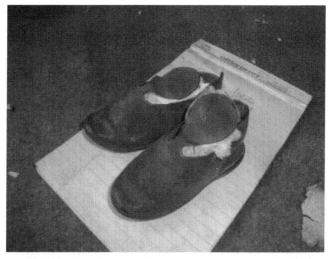

This picture reminds us that God can do anything!

God is our refuge and strength, a very present help in trouble.
Psalm 46:1

Chapter 8

When We Are The Mountain

Every now and then, we've found, that the mountain we need God to move is actually us! Over the years Dwight and I have laughed as we've talked about some of the things that we intended to do, yet God blocked, in one way or another, the very possibility! We are so thankful that He really is always looking out for our best.

Sometimes our plans are not necessarily "bad" but His plans are always "best"! And yes, through prayer, He has been our Mountain-Moving God, even when we tried to place the mountain there to begin with!

It was 1992 and we had just been called to our very first pastorate near Richmond, Virginia. We could not wait to get there!

Dwight had been an interim pastor at this little rural

church for ten weeks while he finished up seminary in Virginia Beach. Each Sunday morning we would load up our three sleeping kids in the wee hours and drive to this little rural community that we had fallen in love with. After the morning service, we would have lunch and then turn around and head back home. Round trip it was 240 miles – but how we loved the people of that little town. They were wonderful.

After ten weeks of interim preaching, the elders met with Dwight and asked if he would come to be their senior pastor. We eagerly responded, "Yes!" We were thrilled, as we had grown to love these sweet people very much. Our miraculous God had sold our home in Chesapeake (another story in our **Memorial Box**) and now we just needed to find a home in Amelia.

Amelia is a rural community so the options were limited at the time. I remember looking at one house and Dwight couldn't stand in the upstairs. Well that wouldn't work! We already had Abigail, Tyler and Autumn and had also just lost our precious baby John while attending seminary. We really wanted a boatload of kids so we knew we needed to find something with ample room to add more!

On one of our trips to preach we had found a home in the village "For Sale by Owner" and were able to look inside. Dwight really liked it. It's true, it would have worked, but I had always longed to live in the country and we could do that without any effort since we were about to pastor in a rural area. Yet Dwight had dreamy ideas of walking to the church each day to work. I had dreamy ideas of being surrounded by acres of farmland. We prayed for wisdom and direction. We were definitely at a standstill.

The more we talked the more it became obvious that Dwight was stuck on that village home. I was so bummed. I talked to the Lord about it a lot and tried very hard to be quiet and just pray!

After seminary finals, we had gone back to New York to vacation and after a few days we left our three kids with our family and headed back to Virginia to find a home. We ended up staying with one of the elders and his wife while we looked.

After arriving in Amelia we talked to our realtor. He knew we wanted a big home and amazingly enough an enormous old Victorian had just come on the market! Oh my gracious – I was ecstatic!! It needed work, but no biggie – we had done that lots and lots of times in the past! The folks we were staying with thought from the description that it must be the giant Victorian literally around the corner from their home, *right next to the railroad tracks.*

We drove around that night to get a peak at what we would be looking at the next day. Oh! Wow! When they said "next to the railroad tracks" they literally meant next to the railroad tracks - with a hair salon building and parking lot in front of it. The bright side was we wouldn't have to walk far for a haircut!

Dwight's immediate response was, "Not a chance!" Well I couldn't help myself, "But look at the house!!" He thought I was nuts. I thought he was unreasonable. In hindsight, he was totally right but I was so smitten with the architecture I obviously couldn't be rational or see straight!

We went back to the elder's home to spend the night. I was praying like crazy! Maybe the Victorian wasn't right, but could he, please, at least keep an open mind? Because I really, truly, didn't think that the village home was right either.

The guest room at their home had twin beds. As we got ready for bed that night we were quietly arguing about what to do. He was more convinced than ever that the village home was it!! In fact he had phoned the homeowner to set up our appointment for the next day and told her that we would most likely be making an offer after seeing it again.

Oh great! I was so frustrated! It was "perfect" according to him because he would be able to walk to work. Friends, I know my man, and walking to work, albeit it romantic sounding, is not reality. (Bless his heart!)

Again I tried to explain how much work the village house needed!! Lights were dangling from the ceiling, holes had been punched in the cabinetry and there were also floorboards missing. It would be a project as well!

With his rose-colored glasses he had not noticed any of that! Of course with my rose-colored glasses I reasoned that we would just put up a fence to keep the kids away from the tracks and, of course, we would totally get used to the noise of the train!

He was so frustrated that I would even consider the Victorian and I was equally frustrated with him. He thought the noise of the tracks and safety issues would drive us nuts.

I decided to just shut up and pray!! So as I climbed into the twin bed I prayed, "Lord, I want to live in the country. I can't imagine living here and not having acres and acres. You know how I've dreamed about it my whole life!! He is so stinkin' stubborn and bent on that village house and although the Victorian might not be right, I just really believe that the village one isn't right either! Here he is telling the homeowner that it looks like we are going to be making an offer!! So Lord, would you please give us a sign that the village house is not for us? Please Lord!! Block it! Do something to make us know that you have something even better for us!"

At that instant, as I said the words, "Do something to make us know that you have something even better for us!" I heard the Lord whisper, "Like water in the basement!"

I actually giggled softly and silently said, "Yes, like water in the basement!" I had giggled because Virginia had been in a drought – the worst in recent years. There had not been any rain in months! The prospect of water in the basement was preposterous – but God!! After those words from the Lord, I had instant peace. Not kidding. The Lord would work it out some way!

Now as it turns out, I am one of those gals who happen to fall instantly asleep when my head hits the pillow. The last thing I remembered was silently saying, "Yes - like water in the basement!"

The next morning when we woke up, Dwight turned to me and in a not-so-happy tone questioned, "Why didn't you answer me? Were you playing games with me?"

Dumbfounded I questioned, "HUH? What are you talking about?" He continued, "Last night as soon as we climbed into bed the train came by! The windows shook like crazy while the whole house trembled!! When it was done I asked you, 'You think living next to a train tracks would be fun?' and you didn't say a word."

I burst out laughing! I had never heard the train at all. I had fallen asleep that fast!! I had never felt or heard anything. "No babe, I was not playing games!" I responded through laughter, "I just fell sound asleep that fast!" He knows me and couldn't help but laugh!

We got ready and headed to see the houses. We saw the Victorian and realized that we would need a bunch of money to replace things like the ancient octopus furnace, the electrical wiring with it's dangling antique light bulbs; not to mention the railroad tracks. It was fun to look at, but not for us to live in and I had peace about that.

Then we headed to the village home where the homeowner had hidden a key since she was out of town. When we got inside I started pointing out the dangling lights, the hole punched cabinets and, of course, the missing floorboards. Hmmm, he had not noticed any of that before. The house would work, don't get me wrong, but I just knew the Lord had something better suited for our needs and a few of our wants too. Although I pointed out the things that were in need of repair, I still wanted to honor my man and see how the house might work for us, since I wasn't sure what the Lord was doing.

As we stood in the long family room of the village home I mentioned to Dwight, "If we bought this home, I'd really like to put the washer and dryer in here with a closet partition." He was game for that and we set out deciding how we could do that. He questioned, "What size is a normal washer?" I had no clue so he enthusiastically ran to the basement to measure the homeowners.

Twenty-five years later and as I type this I can still hear his footsteps pounding on the wooden basement stairs and his scream! I ran toward the basement door shouting, "WHAT – WHAT???? ARE YOU OKAY?" He was incredulous, "Linny! The basement is flooded!"

At that moment the Lord's words from the night before (which I had forgotten) instantly came back to me! I was stunned as I told him, "Whitey, I was praying last night that the Lord would block us somehow from buying this house if He had something better in mind. He whispered, 'Like water in the basement' and I giggled because you know it's been a drought!! How in the world could there be a flood in the basement?"

When we had looked at the house before it had been dry as a bone and not even musty smelling! Dwight decided to slosh his way through the basement to see if it was from the washing machine, but without a doubt, it was not!

82

What in the world?? To this day there is still no logical explanation, which leaves only ONE explanation. The Lord had given us a clear sign that this was NOT the home for us. How He did it – we'll definitely never know!

Dwight did not hesitate a speck, "Okay Linny, let's get out of here – the Lord has spoken." And Dwight was fine with it. Really, he never looked back! He's my hero! Why settle for 'good' when God's plan is always 'best'?

We ended up buying a cozy, two-bedroom singlewide mobile home (yes, you read that right) nestled on 21 gorgeous acres just about five minutes outside of town. We eventually built a home behind the mobile home and then sold the mobile home and it was pulled off the property.

Our church called us "Green Acres" because we were two city folks turned wanna-be-farmers. We even had an old Ford tractor! Dwight and I would flip to see which one of us would get to bush hog!! Gracious be – we had a blast living there!!

We had half a pond that we shared with our neighbors (Dwight's dream was to have water) and in the woods we had a small creek with a little teeny-tiny falls which we named "little Niagara Falls" since I grew up about thirty minutes from Niagara Falls.

We romped and hiked and played and loved that precious place! There was no doubt the Lord provided it and we knew, once again, that He had moved the mountain *of us* from something that probably would have been good and replaced it with something that was *best*.

The icing on the cake was that the very first morning in our mobile home I awoke to the sound of a rooster in the distance. Those closest to me know that of all the possible things I would want to hear, the sound of a rooster would be at the top of the list! I love roosters! The rooster's crow from our neighbor's farm that very first morning, and every morning after, was definitely a love gift from the Lord just for me! I giggled and grinned each time I heard it. A rooster is still one of my most favorite sounds in the entire world!

Yes, indeed. God moves the mountains, even when they are our own stubborn will, working continually to make way for His very best!

A couple of years ago, while visiting our sweet friends Jerry and AnneMarie, I snapped a picture of that old home we had built. In our Memorial Box is the picture reminding us that His plan is always best.

I will remember the deeds of the LORD;
yes, I will remember
your miracles of long ago.
Psalm 77:11

Chapter 9

"Get to the House!"

When a trauma brings someone close to death, often in the aftermath, there is a sober humbling that the God of the universe would reach down and rescue him or her. This story is one of our rescue stories.

It was May 2003 and we were pastoring in Virginia. I had been teaching a women's morning Bible study. At the end of the year, in appreciation, these sweet women had given me two gift certificates - one for a pedicure and another for lunch with Dwight in Richmond. While Dwight and I were in Richmond enjoying the afternoon, they would come and clean our home for us! Wow – what a three-fold blessing!

After my first-ever pedicure, I met Dwight for lunch. As we parted ways after lunch, Dwight headed further into Richmond to run errands and I headed toward home.

Yet, as I drove toward home I felt a very strong urge that I needed to stop at the cleaners in Richmond and pick up some clothes we had there. I didn't really want to stop, as I am a homebody and couldn't wait to get home to my favorite little people. Yet the Lord's urging was so strong, I stopped.

After parking, I went inside and found the dry cleaner, which was normally empty, full of people waiting. I wanted to turn around and leave, but the urge had been so strong, that I just stood behind the crowd waiting my turn. I noticed that there were two girls working behind the counter. There were never two girls behind the counter and I thought that was odd.

Although the cleaner's waiting area is small, there were probably about eight people waiting in front of me. All of a sudden, in the midst of the busyness of that shop and all the people waiting I heard the one girl working behind the counter turn to her coworker and rather loudly say, "I AM SOOOO SCARED."

Now what you have to understand about me is that I am truly a shy person. Hard to believe that I write about our lives on a very public blog and that I love public speaking, but really, down deep - I am shy. Yet here I was standing behind a group of people I didn't know, waiting my turn and upon hearing that girl say she was scared I questioned over everyone in front of me, "What are you scared of?" I even surprised myself!

The girl heard me and turning, looking over top of the people in front of me, questioned, "Didn't you hear? There is a tornado that is going to hit Amelia in 20 minutes and it will then hit here in 30 minutes."

Our home was in Amelia! My kids were home alone and I was 35 minutes from our home! When she said that, I kind of shrieked, "OH MY GRACIOUS! I live in Amelia and my kids are home alone!" I turned and literally ran out of the cleaners.

Phoning Dwight, I told him about the tornado and asked him if he would please go and get Tyler. Tyler was working at a grocery store in Richmond near the dry cleaner. I would speed home since I was closer to home. Best-case scenario I could be home in 30 minutes, but that was still past the time for the tornado to hit.

I then called Autumn who was almost 14-years-old and had Emma, Graham and Liberty at home with her since my friends had finished cleaning.

Urgently, I explained, "Autumn, you have to remain calm. You must listen. There is a tornado coming toward Amelia. It is supposed to hit in 20 minutes! Please take the kids to the basement to play under the stairs. Make a fort! Take with you some water in a jug, grab some crackers and blankets and do it now! Do not freak the kids out. Just tell them to come quickly. Be as calm as you can while you do it. Take the house phone downstairs with you." Autumn did an outstanding job remaining calm, gathering the supplies and the taking the kids downstairs to play.

I started heading down Hwy 360 toward Amelia. In the distance I could see the clouds getting darker. Within a minute or two, the sky became a gross brown color. The wind became intense. I was praying. Dwight was praying.

It was then that I remembered that my mom lived about 15 minutes from our home so maybe; just maybe, she could get to the kids quickly. I phoned her. She had not heard about the tornado but jumped in her car and sped toward our home. I was so relieved that they would not be alone.

As I drove the wind grew more ferocious and I began to cry out to the Lord to spare my kids. Move the tornado! Do something!! Anything!! The weather grew even more intense with each passing moment as I headed right into it.

I talked with Dwight on my cell constantly, updating him on how horrible the weather was. I was crying as hail balls the size of true baseballs began pelting my car. Dwight urged me to pull over and lay __ down in the ditch.

We had lived in the Southeast for the last 13 years and I knew that there were plenty of snakes - Copperheads for starters so there was no way, no how, that I was climbing in a ditch! Tornado? Copperhead? I'll take the tornado.

It was getting almost impossible to see as I crossed the line into Amelia County. Debris was swirling around and the sky was browner than brown. The hail balls were deafening as hundreds slammed into the car. I was praying out loud at a furious rate!

Realizing the weather was too tumultuous to reach home, I remembered hearing that a little girl who played on Emma's soccer team lived with her family not far off Hwy 360. Her parents had visited our church once and I had spoken to them a couple of times at the soccer games. I felt I should seek shelter with them. Again, this was so out of character for me.

I wasn't sure which little side road they were on. Seeing one road to the right and slowing down to turn, I heard the Lord clearly say, "Not this one." I continued on. Before long I came to the next side road and I felt the Lord say, "Turn here." I turned right and went over the railroad tracks. It was so hard to see, but all of a sudden I recognized their SUV coming down their long driveway toward the dirt road I was on. I turned into their driveway and met them part way.

I didn't know this family, really, not at all. Yet I shouted over the powerful sounds, "Where are you going?" Debbie shouted back, "We are going to check on Gary's parents." I questioned, "Do you have a basement?" She said they didn't. I screamed, "We have to get to an interior room!"

All of a sudden, while Debbie and I were shouting back and forth, Gary screamed at the top of his lungs, "GET TO THE HOUSE!!!" He threw their car into reverse and speeding backward, their car literally disappeared out of sight.

I wanted to get to their house, too, but the swirling items and storm prevented me from seeing exactly where their home was.

Slowly I moved forward while my car was pelted with debris and hail balls. It was relentless! Finally, I spotted the edge of their home and stopped. I strained my eyes and thought I could see Gary waiting in the garage a few feet from where I was parked.

I somehow managed to put the car into park but when I went to get out of the car, because of the terrifying stress, the Multiple Sclerosis in my body had instantly shut my arms and hands down. I literally could not open the car door!

I cried aloud to the Lord, "Please, please, help me Lord!! Open my door!" Groping for the handles with my wrists, I was able to use my fists and wrists to open the door while my hands refused to open or function. I fell out of the car and stumbled toward Gary. Gary hugged me and calmly spoke, "It's going to be all right." His words of comfort were a gift from the Lord. The sound of the wind was incredible!!

Once inside their home, Debbie and I moved their daughters and their two little visiting girlfriends into their half bath. We were shouting back and forth when I realized that I had always heard that a tornado sounds just like a freight train! I was stunned! The wind sounded *exactly* like a freight train!

The four little girls, Debbie and I were huddled together praying and singing loudly as our hearts were racing! It was truly one of the most terrifying times of my life.

After what seemed like an eternity, the air became eerily quiet. We opened the half bath door and stepped out.

Gary met us as Debbie and I learned that when we had been shouting back and forth between our cars Gary had looked in his rear view mirror and actually saw the funnel cloud heading directly toward us. It was then that he had screamed, "Get to the house!" They had not known that a tornado was coming!

A funnel was that close!! It was coming straight down their long tree-lined driveway snapping off the beautiful trees as it blasted through. We had been right in the tornado's path! If we had not moved our cars from the driveway we would have been hit by it!!

We walked outside and stopped. We were speechless! The treetops were gone on their tree line. Their home looked like someone had taken a baseball bat and had batting practice against the sides of it. The once smooth siding was now full of enormous holes. Our car was dented to smithereens from the merciless hail.

Of course while briefly surveying the area all I could

think about were my kids so I hugged them both and hurried toward home, which was still 15 minutes away. As I entered Highway 360 I was shocked to see that there was utter destruction everywhere! Trees were down blocking the road and I could not reach the kids on my cell (the power had gone out and our home phone no longer worked). It had never crossed my mind that if Gary and Debbie's property had been destroyed, it would be the same nearby!

As it was, Dwight had been able to get Tyler from work and they came to pick me up at a little convenience store not far from Gary and Debbie's home. The destruction everywhere was incredible. Our church offices had been hit hard. A gigantic oak had been uprooted and fell, crushing the roof of Dwight's office and landing precisely on his desk and chair! Had Dwight been sitting at his desk instead of Richmond, he would have been killed.

We were finally able to reach home and found Autumn had done an incredible job of calmly moving Emma, Graham and Liberty to safety, bringing both food and water with her. My mom brought sweet reassurance while they waited for the funnel to pass. There was over $17,000 in damages to the siding of our home!

As it turns out Debbie and I had to process the events of the tornado and talked on the phone nearly every day for months. It had been traumatizing for both of us. Huddled together in her half bath while a tornado raged outside turned out to be an absolute blessing from the Lord – He knew how much I needed her. She became one of my closest friends of all time. We would sit on my big rambling front porch sipping cold-coffee concoctions we had invented. We'd make pies together. We'd cook together. She is a treasure and to this day we still call each other: *Twister Sister!*

God's protection was overwhelming that day. What if I had continued driving down Hwy 360 without stopping at the cleaners unaware that a tornado was heading toward me? No doubt one of those giant southern trees could have easily fell on our car. What if Gary had not seen the funnel coming down the tree line? What if Dwight had been in his office? The list goes on. It was His grace to spare us, create a friendship when we least expected it and provide for each of our needs. This is why we call Him Our Miracle-working, Mountain-moving, Awe-inspiring, Gasp-giving God. His protection is magnificent!

In our Memorial Box we have a picture of a funnel cloud to always remind us of His protection.

The righteous person may have many troubles, but the Lord delivers him from them all. Psalm 34:19

Chapter 10

When There Really is No Explanation

It was 1986, our oldest two, Abigail and Tyler were just little tikes, and we found ourselves in need of a new car. Minivans were the newest craze and three-year-old Abigail and Dwight began working me over that we needed one. They kept saying, "Everyone has one!" I wasn't all that interested but they eventually wore me down.

We have worked our entire marriage to stay away from all depreciating debt, so we had been saving for quite a long time for this car purchase. We were bound and determined to buy with cash. We set our budget and promised each other that we would not break it and take a loan. It was then that we began the search. We looked at several dealerships but didn't find "our" van.

A few weeks passed and one day Dwight phoned.

He had found *our* van – he was sure of it! It was at a dealership in a neighboring suburb, it had just arrived on the lot and he wanted me to come see it right then. I asked him how much it was. He told me the price, which was $3,000 over our budget! Hmm. What about the deal to stick to our budget?

He was so excited about this van! It had power windows and power locks, which back in the day, both would be a new treat! I asked him about the $3,000. difference and our promise. He reasoned, "But Linny, it's only $3,000 more and it has power locks and windows!"

I didn't say anything more. He knew me well enough to know that I was not very excited about going into debt – power windows and locks or not! Besides, my man was so excited that he just didn't really want to talk about that "little" $3,000 thing!

In my heart I was not interested in the van at all. We had had a deal about only spending a certain amount and here he was throwing that deal to the wind. What the heck?

At the same time I am a woman whose heart wants to submit in every area to my husband's leadership. So what did I do? I didn't argue with him. I just said, "Okay, I will come look at it."

I loaded my little Abigail and baby boy Tyler in the car and drove across town to the car dealership where he was waiting for us. As I was driving I was pleading with the Lord. I told Him, "We had a deal. He wants to ditch the deal. God you have to do something!! I don't know what but I know that you can be the deal saver! You don't want us in debt either! You can do something to block this – do something, anything! Please Lord!!!"

I had known the Lord to interrupt our lives with His plan so I knew I could trust Him. I was not going to manipulate or control the decision. Dwight, as the head of our home, would make the final decision but in the meantime I would pray like crazy!!

When I got to the dealership he was waiting out front. He was beaming from ear to ear – he was so excited he was almost bouncing. He took me right over to the van because he wanted me to test-drive it. He had already done that before I arrived.

So I climbed in the front seat and went to move the seat forward so I could reach the pedals. Dwight was standing beside me to help me get the levers situated and the seat moved forward. With Dwight being 6'2" he had had the seat way back. He was so tickled pushing the button, moving the seat till it stopped in the most forward position.

Surprisingly my right foot did not reach the gas pedal. It didn't even come close. Dwight tried to lower the seat. Again, my foot did not reach. My foot wasn't almost to the pedal; it was clearly about eight inches away from it. Literally!

Dwight questioned the salesman, "Hey, how do you move the seat closer to the pedal?" The salesman came to our side to help. The man showed him the same buttons that Dwight had already been pushing. He was doing it right, however my right foot would not reach the pedal. No kidding. It wasn't even close to the pedal nor was it "almost" there. My foot would not reach for anything. My legs were just dangling off the seat.

Now two grown men, my sweet hubby and this car salesman, were leaning over trying, pushing, wiggling it all to get that seat to move forward! Nada. Nothing. Not even close.

The salesman had me get out. He jumped in. He tried moving the seat closer, up, down, over - anything to get close enough to that gas pedal. He started mumbling under his breath something like this: "This has never happened before. It's a standard van and standard pedals. Your wife is short, but she's not *that* short. This seat should be able to reach. Someone test drove it yesterday and they didn't have a problem with the seat reaching."

And honestly, I was trying so hard not to cover my elation, I was almost laughing out loud and I was now the one beaming from ear to ear!

After probably 15 minutes of trying to get the seat close enough that my feet would reach the pedals they both gave up. Clearly there was no way we could buy that van when I could not reach the gas pedal. Dwight just said, "That is so weird. I guess we will have to keep looking."

As I drove home with my sweet kiddos I was just laughing and praising the Lord! I have no doubt that if a person, who was the same height as I was, had come to test-drive that same van two minutes after we left their feet would have reached just fine. I am convinced that God did something just for us and no one will ever convince me otherwise.

A few weeks later God provided a wonderful minivan within our budget that served us for many, many years.

Sweet friends, He is the God who can make seats not reach gas and brake pedals so people don't go into debt that they really don't need! He is the God who heard my cries to block it even though I was submitting to my husband's call to come look.

He is the God of the impossible and when there is no explanation then there is only one explanation – our great God who loves to move on our behalf.

**A tiny van rests in our Memorial Box
to symbolize the van and
the depreciating debt He miraculously
kept us from.**

*I will sing to the Lord as long as I live;
I will sing praise to my God while I have my being.
Psalm 104:33*

Chapter 11

The Best Years

Those who hope in Him will not be disappointed!
Isaiah 49:23

Many years ago, as I attempted to describe what God had done in Isaiah's adoption I found most vocabulary words sorely lacking. I longed for words that would describe with incredible magnitude God's miraculous power.

Many, many times over the years we have seen God perform miracles. There have been many mountains that those around deemed "impossible" to move; yet He moved them! There have been situations that He worked with such power that all we could do was to stand in complete awe! And then there have been times

when in one miraculous movement He stepped into the
situation (often while we were yet unaware) and
divinely orchestrated each precision movement so that
the only thing we could do was gasp!

One day the phrase came to me and it has stuck ever
since: **God is truly our Miracle-Working, Mountain-
Moving, Awe-Inspiring, Gasp-Giving God!!** There is
nothing that He cannot or will not do for those He loves!!
He merely says the word and it is done!

Our **Memorial Box** is full of stories that fit into most
of these categories – all are miraculous just because of
who God is! But some have caused us to gasp, some
have caused us to stand in awe and others have caused
us to weep tears of joy for years to come at the very
mention of the mountain He moved.

In fact if you ask our son Isaiah "What has God done
for you?" without hesitation he will answer, "He moved
the mountains!" Yes, indeed. God moved the mountains
on behalf of our son and talking about it causes my eyes
to well with tears every single time.

This **Memorial Box** story really begins in November
of 2005. It had been a season filled with all kinds of
changes for our family.

Let me just start by saying, I love being a mom.
There is nothing I love more. I remember back in
elementary school in the early 60s, the teacher would

inevitably begin each school year by having the students go around the room and tell, one by one, what they dreamed of being when grown.

Most girls answered, "I want to be a teacher." Occasionally one would say, "I want to be a nurse." But I was the only one who would quietly respond, "I just want to be a mom." I was usually embarrassed because I was shy to begin with, but people would stare at me as if to say, "A mom? That's the dumbest idea ever!"

But I couldn't help it. It was my only dream. I always wanted to have 18 children and I wanted them lovingly gathered from around the world. While growing up I longed to have a dollhouse and since that never happened, I drew on paper an aerial view which exposed all the rooms. There were several bedrooms, filled with 18 beds and each bed had a name on it!!

So in late 2005, my heart was grieving. Our oldest, Abigail, had left a few years earlier to attend college followed by a move to California. Our second oldest, Tyler, had recently left to pursue his dreams of a military career and our 3rd oldest, Autumn had graduated and moved to do mission work in Nepal and India with YWAM. The three big kids being gone had left a huge hole in my heart!

Yes, yes. I understand. This is what we raise our children to do, but we don't have to like it! My heart cried a lot. I just couldn't imagine having these last three that were still at home moving out as well. And yes, I was spending a lot of time lamenting to the Lord about how sad I was. I even said to Him on several occasions in the stillness of the night, "Oh Lord. I feel like the best years of my life are behind me!"

It's not in my DNA to share things like this with anyone else. Most mornings I get out of bed while everyone is sleeping and go to spend time alone with the Lord. I read my Bible, pray, meditate on His word, and whisper my deepest secrets, needs and feelings. He listens faithfully, cares about each thought and feeling I have and the best perk of all - He never, ever tells anyone else! And He had indeed heard several times from me, "I feel like the best years of my life are behind me!" The words were coming from deep within my soul. I was nearly distraught!

And so it was that in November of 2005, Dwight and I were attending a meeting of our staff and volunteers at the church we pastored. As the meeting drew to a close, I was on the stage beside my husband who was finishing up the meeting with prayer.

The meeting finished and still on the platform, I noticed our newest staff pastor, Benjie, coming into the sanctuary from the back door. The second I saw his face the Lord whispered to me, "The word Benjie is about to give you is a prophetic word directly from me!" As His whisper came to my soul, simultaneously, Benjie maneuvered through the crowd with purpose, glancing up toward me as he headed straight to where I stood.

Benjie, along with his wife Megan, were new to our staff and Dwight and I were looking forward to getting to know them better. As I waited, I just couldn't even begin to imagine what Benjie was about to tell me. Now beside me, he spoke hesitantly, "Umm, I feel like the Lord wants me to tell you something." I assured him I was ready!

Benjie continued, *"He wants you to know that the best years of your life are ahead of you!"* I literally gasped! The *exact* words that I had been crying out to the Lord were now being repeated back to me, with a promise!! I was completely dumbfounded!!! I was so stunned as I had never told anyone. Not one soul. No one. I hadn't written it anywhere. It was a secret between the God of the Universe and I. And here, because of God's miraculous grace, a young man, who I barely knew, was telling me that God was giving me a promise - *the best years of my life were ahead of me!*

I was giddy when I heard the words!! Literally bouncing for joy! I instantly replied to Benjie, "Then we must be going to adopt at least seven more kids in order to be the *best* years because right now we have six –

"best" would mean *at least* seven more!" Benjie kind of laughed. I'm sure that *at least seven* **more** kids would not be everyone's dream, but it was mine! There was clearly nothing else on my mind and the Lord knew it! I desperately longed for more treasures! A giant pile more! Our table overflowing! A boatload! A bucket full!! Toothbrushes everywhere! The laundry piled sky high! And laughter, lots and lots of laughter!

What struck me that night as I pondered this precious promise from the Lord was that God was in the future. He knew exactly what the plan would be and I was 100% confident it meant at least seven more – after all it was going to be *the best* – which to me meant even better than our very spectacular gathering of six!

I never again lamented about the big kids leaving home and the house being too quiet because it was going to be full once more! I also didn't try to figure out how God was going to add to our family. I have slowly learned that if the Lord says it, He is going to do it and He's already set the plan in motion, even if we can't see it! I just needed to trust Him and His promises!! Of course, I couldn't wait to see what He had in store because it was going to be *the best!* Wow!! This was just crazy-miraculous!

Six months later we found ourselves at our annual pastor's convention. It was a special time each year for all the pastors, in our denomination, to gather together. This particular year it was held in Washington DC.

While attending the convention Dwight, the kids and I decided to wander the exhibit hall along with our close friends, Nick and Robin. We rarely get to see them and when we do, we usually laugh lots. I will never forget rounding the corner of one aisle and seeing a gigantic banner of Chinese children! My heart leapt at the precious orphan's faces!

Hurrying to the man at the booth I mourned, "Oh if only we were younger, we would totally adopt from China!" He responded, "Recently China has lowered their age restrictions, I'm certain you would not be too old! How old are you?" I told him that I was 48 and my husband was 52. He assured me that we were not too old!

I turned on my heels in record time and literally ran to where Dwight was standing laughing with his buddy Nick. (They really do laugh all the time!) Grabbing Dwight by the arm I emphatically tugged his arm back and forth squealing loudly, "Whitey!! Whitey!! They said we're not too old! China has changed their regulations, our age is okay!"

At that moment, there is no doubt that our powerful God was doing something dramatic in our lives. It could not be denied. I gathered the information from the gentleman and within an hour was on their website looking at the precious faces of Chinese orphans whose files they held.

The agency had a picture list of the children with a tiny write-up about each one. Our daughter Emma was looking with me. As we looked at each face, tears kept welling in our eyes. They all were so precious, each face beautiful beyond words, all in need of a family and all had special needs.

When I opened the picture of one little guy though, it was different. There he was! I knew it! He was ours. I could not stare at his face without dripping tears. His face was calling to us. We needed him!

I noticed immediately that this precious little boy's shirt had on it the word "found" (upside down) in English as well as a bold, 'Bye"! Yes, this was our son. I reasoned, we had "found" him and one day he would say "Bye" to orphanage life! I just knew it.

As we looked at the little write-up, we also found this picture of him. He looked scared in this picture. I felt his eyes were calling to us: Can you love me?

Later I showed his picture to Dwight. He, too, was smitten. We decided to pray in earnest. Could this little guy be the one the Lord had for our family? In my heart I knew that I knew that I knew. But yes, we would pray.

By the time we got home from the convention there were words above this little guy's picture. They read, "File to be Sent Back." I told Dwight what the site said and he told me to call the agency and ask what that meant.

The woman who answered the phone explained that it meant that soon his file would be returned to China and sometimes that would be the end of the attempt at finding him a family. I was sick!

I called Dwight at the church office and told him what she had said. He told me to call her back and tell her we wanted him!! He continued, "This little guy is ours!! We have to get him home!" Ahhh, I love that man of mine!! His heart is tender to the plight of the orphan and he's willing to live like he means it!

Phoning her back I told her what my husband had said and suddenly remembering my health, my first question was, "I have Multiple Sclerosis. Can we still adopt him? Will China be okay with that?" That was, to me, the only possible obstacle to bringing him home since the man at the convention booth had said our age was fine.

She answered without hesitation, "Having MS is no problem with China, we will just have to disclose it to them. We even have a couple that recently adopted and one parent is a quadriplegic and China was fine. We just

111

have to disclose it." Whew! So thankful!! He was ours for sure!! I knew it!! My heart had already been broken in a million pieces for him!

With Chinese adoptions, each potential adoptive family is required to send an immediate Letter of Intent (also called a LOI). A LOI is the submission of a simple medical form, brief financials and a small statement as to why we wanted to adopt this little guy. Easy-peasy.

After we had sent the paperwork in, China would review it and likely issue us a "PA" which stood for Pre-Approval. Pre-Approval means that they are tentatively saying they accept you as the parents of this child. Tentatively because they will be going over everything with a fine-tooth comb once our official Dossier arrived in China. The Dossier is an enormous compilation of paperwork including our home study, our financials, letters of reference, in-depth medical, all certified and authenticated at the state level, federal level and Chinese consulate level. It is very detailed and every piece has to be done with extreme care.

At the time, I was working part-time as a Biblical counselor on staff at our church. After my last counseling appointment one day, I pulled out the rest of the necessary paperwork to fill out for China in order to submit our LOI (Letter of Intent).

It's crazy how we can remember significant things, isn't it? I was working away and came to a line on the medical form that said, "Current Health". There was a blank beside it and the agency paperwork stated that I write "Good" in that blank. At that moment, the Lord seemed to whisper, "Call and ask if this is where you are to disclose that you have MS." But I reasoned, "They know I have MS. If this were the place where I am to disclose it, they would have not told me to put "Good" for my health. They must have meant in the full medical history that is part of the dossier. Besides their offices are already closed back east."

I finished up the necessary paperwork. Before long we had the papers all notarized and sent off to the agency for translation. Within a couple of weeks we had word that China had indeed granted us Pre-Approval for this sweet little guy whose face had screamed, "I belong to you!"

As we began to work on the gobs of detailed paperwork for the dossier we dreamed of that little guy coming home to us. Each day we talked of all the things we would do with him once he was home. We had placed his picture in the midst of all the individual pictures of each of our children. He was ours. We knew it. We needed him far more than he needed us and we couldn't wait for him to be in our arms.

The agency that held our son's file and was doing the processing for his adoption did not do home studies in our area. By God's grace, the agency that came up when we searched for a home study provider in our area was Chinese Children International Adoption Agency based in Denver, Colorado. Little did we know that Chinese Children was not only the largest facilitator of Chinese adoptions in the United States, but they also have an impeccable reputation for each adoption they facilitate! We were completely unaware that God was orchestrating each step behind the scenes!!

As we were gathering all the necessary documents for the dossier we, of course, had our doctor fill out the necessary paperwork for our medicals. He fully disclosed the MS and the other autoimmune disorders I have. We carefully had each piece of the paperwork authenticated by the local, state and United States government as well as the Chinese consulate. It was a long, tedious process.

At the same time, we began to search for a name for our son. We knew Isaiah was a prophet in the Old Testament and we also found that the name means, "Salvation by the Lord". The meaning of a name is very important to us and we knew that Isaiah's name was powerful. We chose his middle name to be "Samuel" after the son of Hannah from the Old Testament book of

I Samuel. Hannah had longed for a baby and God heard her heart's cry and answered! Samuel means "God has heard" and it seemed perfectly appropriate for this little 2-1/2 year old bundle of joy that this mama's heart had been desperately longing for. Indeed! God had heard!

With our dossier finally off to China we settled in to wait. As months passed, we heard nothing and I began to grow concerned. What was taking so long?? China had given Pre-Approval so quickly yet we had now been waiting for our Letter of Acceptance much longer than it seemed we should. Finally, after waiting for months I phoned our agency and I questioned if they were concerned. The woman who had helped from the very first phone call came on the line and said that sometimes it was taking a little longer than the usual amount of time and there was no need to be alarmed.

A few weeks later we found ourselves flying to the East Coast to see our oldest son graduate from yet another specialized training in the military. As the Lord would have it, I had to go to my office for an appointment with a client the day before we left. After I was finished, I was hurrying to get packed up and Benjie stopped at my office door.

He explained that he felt the Lord wanted him to tell me something *before* we left on our trip. After the word from the Lord through Benjie the previous year, I couldn't wait to hear. Benjie then reached into his pocket and pulled out a piece of paper. He handed me the little note and explained that as he was in prayer that morning the Lord had directed him to write this scripture reference down and to make sure he gave it to me *before* our trip.

On it was written: Psalm 105:19. I stepped back to my desk, opened my Bible and read:

Until the time came to fulfill his dreams,
the LORD tested Joseph's character."

I would love to say that my heart was filled with joy, peace and comfort as I read the words of the verse. However, as I read it, I literally felt sick to my stomach. This scripture is referring to Joseph (from the book of Genesis). Joseph had been his father Jacob's favored son, yet because of his father's favored treatment of him, his stepbrothers had burned with jealousy. One day, Joseph told his brothers about a dream he had had where he actually ruled over them. That infuriated his brothers and they already hated him! Unbeknownst to his father, his jealous brothers seized an opportunity to grab Joseph and immediately sold him as a slave. Joseph was subsequently carried off to a distant land to live.

Joseph's life was one of painful rejection, horrific betrayal and crushing heartache. Eventually he was falsely accused and convicted of a crime he didn't commit and spent years in prison. Then, against all odds, Joseph was restored to a position of powerful authority in the very same land where he had served prison time!

There is no doubt that Joseph's life had to have been unimaginably difficult. Although Joseph, by human standards, had every right to be angry, many years later he actually was given the opportunity to determine the fate of the very brothers who had betrayed him years earlier. Even with all the pain, rejection and life-altering events that his brothers had inflicted on Joseph, he had the strength to issue them astounding grace and shower them with mind-boggling forgiveness, bountiful blessings and lavish love.

Joseph actually told them not to quarrel amongst themselves for their painful actions toward him years earlier!! He explained that the very situations that they had intended to harm him with had actually enabled God to move him into a place where he would be able to one day save their lives!!

I know Joseph's story well as it is the one I have studied most of my life. It is a powerful historical fact and Joseph is one of my personal heroes. I can't wait to

117

meet him one day in heaven!! I am certain that the forgiveness that Joseph issued has encouraged many a person to do the same over the years!! True to the prophetic dream Joseph had had many years earlier, he one day ruled over his brothers.

So the day Benjie shared the verse about Joseph with me…I felt sick. Yes, God had prevailed (as He always does) in Joseph's life and the prophetic dream had indeed come to pass! However, in between the dream and the fulfillment of the dream Joseph had endured many years of dreadful heartache. Although the verse brought hope, it was difficult to swallow knowing Joseph's years between the promise given and the promise fulfilled.

Anyway, we left the following day to head to the East coast to see our son graduate. The first few days were filled with joy as we spent time together as a family. We are so very proud of our son's sacrifice for our great nation! The last full day we decided to do a little shopping. Dwight had taken a few of the kids into the bookstore as I headed into TJ Maxx with some of the girls. As we browsed around my cell phone rang. I looked at the caller ID and saw that it was the adoption agency. In my heart I felt kind of anxious – no doubt the Lord had been preparing me.

After saying hello, the voice that greeted me on the other end responded seriously, "I want you to know Linny that this call is being recorded and I also have someone in the room to listen to this call." The voice speaking was the very same woman who had helped me many times in the past yet she was no longer warm, friendly or lighthearted.

Now I felt like throwing up. What was going on? Managing to stammer a feeble, "Okay" as I waited for her to continue. "We are calling to inform you that China has withdrawn your Pre-Approval and they will not be allowing you to adopt your son."

My mind was reeling as so many thoughts were spinning around inside me! Why would China be doing this? I was stunned, completely speechless. Finally I questioned, "Why? What happened? How could they do this?"

She proceeded, "Well you should have notified them in the Letter of Intent that you had Multiple Sclerosis. They saw in your full medical paperwork in your dossier that you have MS and they feel that you are trying to sneak it in without notifying them up front."

I was in complete shock as I struggled for words, "What can we do? How do we explain to them the situation? I run and exercise every day. I really am in 'good' health."

Her answer was simple and direct, "There is no appeal process. It's over. Move on with your life. You are going to have to just forget about him."

I was in complete shock!! Forget about Isaiah Samuel? Are you kidding me?? He wasn't a chair that we had wanted for our family room that had sold out and was now being discontinued. He was our son!! His handsome picture hung on several of our walls. His name was already listed in a special name frame our friend Mitzi had bought! We had been praying for him for months!! Our hearts were fully invested!! There was no way we were forgetting about him or moving on!! That idea was the most absurd thing I had ever heard!! Forget about him? Are you kidding me? What a completely ridiculous suggestion!!

I told her that Dwight was in another store and I asked that she would tell him when I found him. Heading next door to the bookstore, I handed him the phone as tears began streaming down my cheeks. Dwight took the phone from me as I stumbled out the door and fell into a heap on the sidewalk outside the bookstore. The kids were now gathered around me sobbing, I was sobbing and we were inconsolable.

On a side note, the sweet little military town where all this transpired touched our souls that day. Of course in the midst of uncontrollable grief we were completely

120

oblivious to what anyone around us would think.

Sitting on the sidewalk we were a hysterical mess. Dwight was still inside the store talking as a car pulled up and the woman on the passenger side asked if she could help. I just shook my head side to side sobbing unable to even respond. Soon a truck pulled up and an older couple got out and asked if they could help. Much later I realized that living in a military base town, they likely thought we had just heard of the loss of a loved one.

When Dwight came out he took me in his arms and the kids wrapped their arms around us. We were one hugging, wailing pile. At that moment Dwight began to pray. I don't remember much of his prayer, but I do remember him repeating what Job once prayed in Job 13:15, "Though you slay us, yet will we trust you."

Limp with grief, Dwight helped me walk to the car. Suddenly, as we neared our car I halted in my steps and shouted while choking back sobs, "Dwight! Do you remember the verse Benjie gave me the other day? This is exactly what it's about. God is going to come through. Isaiah is a promise for us. God is going to get him home. I have no idea how, but God always keeps His promises!"

**Isaiah's first picture sits inside
our Memorial Box to remind us of
the promise of the BEST years.**

*Until the time came to fulfill his dreams,
the LORD tested Joseph's character."
Psalm 105:19*

Chapter 12

Where a Mountain Once Stood

Once in the car we called our family and friends and pleaded with them to start to pray. Dwight called our staff to tell them.

The rest of the day we continued to cry, pray and talk. What could we do? Yes, our agency had said to 'forget about him" but there was not a chance we would ever consider such nonsense!! We didn't know what we would do, but forgetting about Isaiah was not an option. No way, no how, never, ever, ever!

The next day our very sober family made their way to the airport and flew across the country. Benjie had phoned Dwight and asked if when we reached home we could come down to talk with our staff at the office.

When we got to the church Benjie took charge, which was a beautiful blessing. We were still reeling! Benjie asked us to explain the situation so they would understand it clearly and then he firmly stated, "We must intercede and ask God exactly what we should be praying. What is the spiritual root of China's decision?"

Friends let me interject; I believe that asking God what is at the root of a situation is probably some of the wisest words ever spoken!! God promises that He whispers secrets to those who fear Him (Psalm 25:14). Why wouldn't He want to give us the strategy for this battle? We can't pray through the battle if we don't understand what the enemy is doing.

Let me make it clear, the enemy was not China but Satan himself! Satan does not want orphans in families where they will heal from loss, trauma and rejection and find acceptance, joy, healing and the unconditional love of family.

So we began to pray and ask God what was at the root of China's reversal. God graciously showed us that China had been offended that we had not provided the MS diagnosis during the LOI paperwork. Offense is rooted in pride. We now felt we knew how to specifically pray.

That day we drove home from the prayer time with our staff and remembered that Chinese Children had done our home study. Knowing that they are the largest facilitator of Chinese adoptions we decided to call them and ask if they might have any insight.

Dwight spoke to Hillary on the phone. She admitted, "There is no formal appeal process with China, however, that does not mean you cannot appeal their decision anyway!!" Hillary was amazing!! She gave us a battle plan! She emphatically told us that we needed to call our agency and insist on speaking only with the director. She gave a very specific strategy for each step the director should take.

Our agency would also need to write a formal letter of apology and include in the letter that I had indeed asked, from our very first phone call, if the MS would be a problem and that I had never tried to deceive our agency, our social worker, China or anyone else. While praying Dwight and I also had the idea of submitting a DVD of both of us jogging and riding our bikes. They would then be able to see that we both really were in "good" health and I was not debilitated despite having MS. We asked Hillary what she thought. She loved the idea!

Hillary also told us that we would need our social worker, Liv, to write a powerful letter on our behalf. She said she would contact her. Hillary told us that time was of the essence and we needed to work fast! We cannot ever thank Hillary enough for her wisdom!! God was working through her - we just knew it. She also said, "There are no promises, but you never know! But you must work fast!" Her words offered us hope and that was very comforting!

We continued to storm heaven for God's wisdom, direction and His clear intervention as Dwight phoned the director of our agency. The director was a very tenderhearted man who has since moved his large adoptive family overseas to serve the orphan. He sincerely loves the orphan and there is no doubt that he was grieved by this situation. Without hesitation he eagerly agreed to help in any way he could! He also agreed to do all that Hillary from Chinese Children had said was needed.

Our close friend and staff member, Seth, had a gift for putting together music with video and filmed me jogging in the park, riding my bike with Dwight and both of us together asking China to reverse their decision. In the video Emma, Graham and Liberty showed Isaiah's picture hanging on the wall and the toys already bought for him. Through tears they pleaded for China to please let Isaiah come home to us.

Our social worker, Liv, wrote a powerful kick-butt letter on our behalf. She emphatically confirmed that I had never tried to hide the Multiple Sclerosis diagnosis.

126

Carefully, yet urgently, each piece of the appeal was put together with intention and sent within days to our agency. They immediately sent it on to China.

That horrific phone call telling us that China had withdrawn their Pre-Approval had come on March 19th. Our formal (although not formal) appeal was sent to China about a week later. **The wait began.**

While our hearts were in agony, we heard from some familiar with Chinese adoptions. What they said did not encourage us at all! Quite the opposite! (Help me understand, why do people sometimes feel they need to share the worst story they know with someone going through something similar?)

During our wait, some of the things we heard from people "in the know" were: "China will never change their mind." "We heard of this happening to someone else and China would not change their mind." "China has too much pride. It doesn't matter what you do, they will never change their mind."

A woman in our church called me a couple of weeks after our devastating phone call and after asking how I was doing responded with, "You are making such a big deal out of this. I'm surprised you are still talking about it. You just need to move on and forget about him!"

I shook my head in disbelief. Our agency's phone call had led our family into one of the darkest seasons of our lives and she was wondering why I was grieving and hadn't moved on? I'm still baffled. She clearly would have been a good substitute on the team with "Job's Comforters". No doubt, in life we have all met those people who just don't know when to keep their lips pressed tightly together. I debated giving her super glue for Christmas. Kidding, of course.

On our end, we thought of little else. How could we? This news looked like the death of a dream. Our hearts were fully invested! The appeal was in and we would not give up. We had also decided that if the appeal didn't work, Dwight would fly to China and meet with whomever he needed to meet with.

But until we heard a response from China about our appeal, we prayed, we fasted and we cried. Sleep was difficult at night. Dwight, the kids and I talked about it all over and over and over. We begged God. We prayed long hours. We fasted some more.

My prayer partner was a precious young woman named Chelsea. Each Thursday we would meet at the crack of dawn at a local coffee shop. While sipping coffee we would share our hearts and then pray together for specific personal needs. As we waited for China to respond, Chelsea asked if Dwight and I would mind her going before our church during all three services to ask everyone to join in a church wide fast for China to reverse their decision. Being firm believers in the power of not only private but also corporate fasting, we eagerly responded, "Yes!" When she presented the idea, many joined in.

As the days wore on we heard nothing. The beginning of April, mid-April and as the end of April neared I was feeling weary, frustrated and very overwhelmed with it all. One Wednesday toward the end of April I announced to Dwight, "I am going into my prayer closet. I am not coming out until I hear from God. I need to know what He is going to do."

I was not kidding. I couldn't take it anymore. The wait was agonizing. I needed to know what was going to happen!!

Gathering my beloved Bible, water, a pillow for sitting on, a pen, my journal and a big box of Kleenex I settled onto our bedroom closet floor. I was not leaving until I heard what God was going to do for our Isaiah.

I was very grateful that I had already been fasting that day, as I tend to hear the Lord much more clearly when I am fasting. In the solitude of our bedroom closet I read my Bible, wept with reckless abandon and pleaded with the Lord to whisper to me what He was doing on Isaiah's behalf.

The Bible declares that God is close to the brokenhearted (Psalm 34:18), that He catches our tears in His bottle (Psalm 56:8) and that He hears our cries and comforts us (Psalm 10:17). He truly cares about our heartache and there's no doubt that our pain was excruciating.

After hours in the closet, I heard His soft whisper. It went something like this: *"Linny, you know I love the orphan. I brought you to the convention to find him. Would I dangle his face in front of you and then snatch it back as if it was all a joke? Not a chance!! Do I just tease you with good things? Do I merely taunt my loved ones? Do you really think I would show you Isaiah's face, have you fall in love with him and then yank him back to an orphanage life forever? Never!! I will come through with every promise for Isaiah! I never go back on promises. I love Isaiah more than you can imagine. Look back over every single detail of Isaiah's adoption to this point. Have I failed you in any way? I will not fail you or Isaiah now. You need to trust me! I always keep my promises! Your hope has to be in me and only me."*

The moment He whispered I felt enormous relief. Isaiah would come home. I had zero idea how - but he would come home! Hope rose up within me like I don't ever remember having before. I knew that I knew that I knew that Isaiah would come home!!

We could not do one thing. It was completely up to the Lord. He would do it. He was our *only* hope! Doubt was history!! Fear was no longer present. I knew my God would come through!! I had no idea how God was going to do it, but I was 100% confident He would!!

Although it is hard to put into words because it is so personal for me, suffice it to say that that time in my prayer closet was a pivotal point in my personal walk with the Lord. I would never be the same! When I came out of our bedroom that day I remember telling Dwight, "God is bringing him home. I have no idea how but He will do it! If need be, He may just complete the paperwork and drop Isaiah in the middle of our family room, I have no clue, but Isaiah will come home to us!" And I meant it with everything in me. There was not even a fiber of doubt!

The next day was Thursday and I could hardly wait to tell Chelsea what God had whispered to my soul. As we sat sipping coffee I explained the events of the previous day and how I no longer was consumed with panic, doubt or fear. God had spoken clearly and powerfully. Chelsea enthusiastically spoke, "Oh Linn! That reminds me of the verse "Those who hope in me will not be disappointed." (Isaiah 49:23) Yes! That was it! My hope was only in the Lord and He would never disappoint!! From that moment on I whispered Isaiah

49:23 day in and day out. *Those who hope in Him will not be disappointed!*

I now could worship joyfully - that adorable, dimple-cheeked little guy was our son and we would have him in our arms before long because the God of the Universe doesn't go back on His promises!

April ended with no news. By God's grace I was able to remain steadfast, unwavering. Then on May 5th, 2007 I received an email from a ministry I had been following. A man with a prophetic gifting had spoken a powerful word to the thousands of recipients on his email list.

The prophetic word went something like this, "May is going to be a month of unprecedented miracles! Those awaiting promises will be given great favor! The Lord will move this month of May in a miraculous way on your behalf! May will be a month of favorable announcements!!"

I was giddy! I knew this was a confirming word from the Lord for our situation. I could hardly wait to tell Dwight when he got home from the church that day!

Later that day, as I shared the prophetic email with Dwight I remember saying, "Babe I know this is from the Lord. I am 100% sure that we will hear 'Yes!' from China in the month of May. It may be May 31st a few minutes before midnight, but we will hear in the month of May."

Those who hope in Him will not be disappointed!

May was a flurry of activity and before long we packed our bags to travel back East to see our son graduate again from another highly specialized training. Interestingly enough, we would be in the same military city where we had received the dreadful phone call on March 19th!!

Spending time together as a family with our son and watching his graduation was a beautiful privilege. Our oldest son loves his younger siblings and so we all were reveling in the precious time together!!

Crammed into the two little adjoining hotel rooms, early on the morning of May 29th, 2007 my cell phone woke us. Opening just one eye I looked to see the caller ID and saw our agency's phone number. I sat up with a start! I was now instantly wide-awake!

Quickly answering, "Hello", I heard the same voice of the woman who had 71 days earlier told me that China was changing their mind. However, this time her voice was not somber, it was sing-songy as she began, "Guess what?" I could hardly contain myself, "WHAT?" She giggled softly and responded with joy, *"China has reversed their decision!!* They said you could bring your son home! China said 'YES!'"

Tears spilled from my eyes as I shouted with giggling joy to Dwight who, of course, was now awake beside me. **"China said, 'Yes!' China said, Yes!'"** He was laughing and crying at the same time!

She explained that the Letter of Acceptance would be coming soon. I can't remember much from the rest of the conversation I was just too overcome with so many emotions! We were a mess!! Crying, laughing and throwing our hands up in shouts of praise!!

I remember running to the adjoining room and trying to tell the kids that the agency had called, but my words were getting all jumbled up with tears and giggling! Dwight had to tell them and then together we all knelt in praise at how our faithful God had powerfully moved the mountain that stood between Isaiah and our family.

Almighty God had prevailed!! He had moved on the entire communist government to reverse their decision!! He had done what many said was impossible! He had shown His might, His power, His authority and His matchless love for one little orphan boy!

Those who hope in Him will not be disappointed!

That day I looked out of our hotel room and saw that across the street was the very shopping plaza where we had sat in a heap sobbing our eyes out just 71 days earlier.

We are pretty sure that aerodynamics had nothing to do with the way our plane flew home that day. It was buoyed by our joy from the miraculous move of our ever-faithful God!!

Less than 2 weeks later our agency had our Letter of Acceptance in hand, which they overnighted to us to sign. When the agency called to tell us that they had received the hard copy of the LOA they mentioned that they were surprised how quickly it had arrived after the verbal reversal. The day they called to say they had our LOA in their hands marked 12 weeks exactly from the day China said "no".

Later I remarked about the timing of it being exactly 12 weeks to our close friend, Dan, who is very gifted in Biblical knowledge. I had found it so intriguing that it was 12 weeks to the day. He responded that it did not surprise him at all that it was exactly 12 weeks from the dreadful "no" to the joyful arrival of the official Letter of Acceptance. He explained that in scripture the number 12 has great significance as it represents *God's divine authority.*

No doubt, God's divine authority had had the final word and His authority has the power to reign over any governmental authority – whether communist or not!

With the final processing of the LOA along with the last of the immigration paperwork, we were given permission to fly to China on August 2nd, 2007.

When we reached the orphanage on August 4th, Isaiah was outside playing at a tiny swing set with another little boy. He turned to see our car arrive and excitedly ran beaming from ear to ear toward us. We were able to snap a picture as he ran, grinning, to our car!

Tears were spilling from all our eyes as we climbed out of the car. He hurriedly grabbed and hugged Graham first! Big brother was thrilled to finally have his little brother!

I could hardly see the joyful meeting because my eyes were swimming in boatloads of tears. He was ours! God had prevailed, just as He said He would.

A copy of Isaiah's official
"Letter of Acceptance"
is in our Memorial Box to remind
us all that where a mountain once stood
is a handsome young boy named Isaiah!

"Those who hope in Him will not be disappointed!"
Isaiah 49:23

Chapter 13

The Seemingly Small Stuff

"Cast all your cares upon Him, for He cares for you." I Peter 5:7

While praying about which stories to include in **The Memorial Box** I felt the need to share simple stories as well as stories that would be deemed remarkable. I desperately desire that each person understand that God cares about *every single detail* of our lives. He longs to be intimately involved in the simple cares as well as the enormous needs.

Looking back over my life I am reminded of a sunny day in October 1969. I was out on our front porch when the woman who lived across the street saw me and invited me to come over to talk with her. Mrs. Franklin and her husband had moved in a few months earlier and the extent of interaction between her and I, up until that point, had merely been waving back and forth. Definitely curious, I ventured over to her home to talk to her. She was about my grandma's age.

Mrs. Franklin's front door was open so I knocked quietly on the screen door. She came to the door smiling and invited me inside gesturing for me to sit down on her couch. This pretty little lady then sat down across from me.

Mrs. Franklin explained that she was looking for someone to clean her home on Fridays for about an hour each week. She was wondering if I would be interested. She detailed what she wanted done: scrub the kitchen and bathroom floor on my knees; wash the baseboards in the living room, hallway, bathroom and both bedrooms; vacuum the living room and both bedrooms; scrub the bathroom sink, tub and toilet; wash the mirror in the bathroom.

The pay would be $2 and she guessed I would be able to get it all done in about an hour. She also said she would train me exactly how she wanted each job done. To an almost eleven-year-old, hard-working and conscientious girl, I was tickled. Mostly tickled because it meant Mrs. Franklin trusted me to come into her home and do a good job. I smiled big and told her I would be happy to work for her. The following Friday I eagerly ventured over to Mrs. Franklin's home. She stayed near me that first day as she showed me exactly what she expected.

I particularly remember how she poured the Murphy Oil Soap in the pan for me to wash the baseboards. I had never seen Murphy Oil Soap before and thought it smelled heavenly! In fact the almost eleven-year-old in me thought it smelled good enough to taste! Don't worry, I didn't partake but the thought crossed my mind more than once over the years! About an hour later, after finishing up all the tasks, Mrs. Franklin handed me two one-dollar bills and reminded me that she wanted me to come back the following Friday. I was so pleased! I had my first job!

Stepping off the curb and crossing the street I noticed that our family car was in the driveway already, which meant my father was home from work. It was too early for him to be home and I hurried to see what was going on.

Opening the back door, I found my mom and dad standing in the kitchen. My mom turned to me and explained, "Your father was laid off today." My dad had worked as a tool and die draftsman at the same company for 24 years. He was a diligent worker: always early, never sick, and a loyal employee. Instantly I felt sick to my stomach.

He told me that just after 4:00pm the owner of the company had walked over to his desk to tell him that his nephew had just graduated from college and would be replacing my dad. My father could clear his desk out and take his last paycheck.

As I went to my room, I was struck with the timeliness of starting to work for Mrs. Franklin. As I began my first day of work at Mrs. Franklin's, my dad had been laid off. This was not a coincidence, not at all. I was confident that it was my faithful God meeting a need before I even knew the need existed.

Of course the $2 each week I earned was not going to provide for our family, but from that day forward I paid for everything I needed. I bought my own clothes, toiletries and had my fund for "fun" from the time I was almost eleven until I married at nineteen.

My first job was, of course, working for Mrs. Franklin. When I was a bit older I began to babysit for people in our neighborhood. At age 14, when it was almost unheard of, I started a paper route on a long street about three blocks from my home. Six days each week I would pull a wagon overflowing as I walked back and forth delivering *The Buffalo News*. Winter was an especially snowy treat! Friends who know of my papergirl days should never question why I love Phoenix so much!

After my paper route I got a job at a nursing home where I worked in the kitchen. From Mrs. Franklin's job and every other income I had, I tithed 10% and faithfully saved the remainder. I was a very frugal young girl and also wanted to be a wise steward.

About a year after my dad lost his job (and still had not found another) the junior high youth group at my church was going to Word of Life snow camp in the Adirondack Mountains. The cost was $40.

Inside I groaned when I heard how much it was. I was thrifty and had saved, but not much. There had been needs and so I had been unable to save much. Although I momentarily wondered how I would ever gather $40, I prayed and felt confident that the Lord would have a way for me to get there. Sure enough the God who loves us each so much was again one step ahead. He really is *always* at work around us!

Before long it was announced that someone in our church had issued a proposal to anyone in the youth group: "If you memorize these specific 100 Bible verses listed on this sheet of paper, your way will be paid to Snow Camp!" I was overjoyed! You bet I could memorize! So I spent the next couple of months memorizing the 100 verses on the list. Each time we had more memorized, we would not only recite them to our youth leader but we also had to go back over the ones we had already memorized. By God's grace, I did it and my way was paid in full.

The amazingly beautiful thing about it all was that as an act of love, a generous person reached out to our youth and their kindness allowed myself (and others) to go to Snow Camp. Personally speaking, there really wouldn't have been any other way. In order to have my way paid, I hid 100 Bible verses in my heart forever. That would be a win in every way! Those verses are treasured within my soul and are still in my memory today.

Now I know that some perhaps, upon hearing about Mrs. Franklin's job and the ability to memorize 100 verses to go to camp, would rather explain it all away as merely coincidental. However, I contend that not seeing God's hand in the little things in each of our lives detracts and blinds our ability to see Him at work in the larger areas.

I am convinced that it was all God and only God. He was continually working on my behalf because I spent my days talking to Him, trusting that He was faithful and believing that He would meet my needs, just like His word said He would.

****

The following story is part of the faith journey Dwight, the kids and I have been walking since moving from Colorado just about six years ago. I share it knowing maybe God has called you or you and your family to do something that would mean a loss of income. Be encouraged! We have seen God do the miraculous when we stepped out in faith.

****

When we brought our little Ruby home from Africa, it necessitated Dwight resigning from senior pastoring in Colorado in order to move to Phoenix for Ruby's neurosurgical needs. It also meant that we would no longer have an income. That could have sounded very scary, but we had had other seasons without an income (like going to seminary and also planting a church). Each previous season God had faithfully provided.

With our move to Phoenix we officially launched our ministry - International Voice of the Orphan - a 501c3 tax exempt ministry. (Our website is IVO.Global) As we took this leap of faith we knew that God would faithfully provide for each of our needs while we devoted our days advocating for the needs of the voiceless orphans in several countries around the world.

144

Shortly after moving to Phoenix, our third oldest, Autumn, and her boyfriend Karl, became engaged. Autumn then asked each of her siblings to be in her wedding. Having seven of her younger siblings still living at home, we knew that God would have to do some mighty things to be able to do that in an affordable way.

As a family we began to pray that God would provide supernaturally for flower girl dresses for Elizabeth, Jubilee and Ruby! Emma, who was still living at home, looked around the web. There were many very pretty dresses – each with a very pretty price tag as well!

Weeks passed, which turned into months. We kept praying. We weren't frantic; we knew He would do something extraordinary if we were patient.

About a month before the wedding, Emma took a couple of our kids to the local thrift store near our home. As Emma was searching one side of the rack, Isaiah was searching the other side. "Hey Emma, look at these!" Isaiah called. Emma ran to look and there they were! Two matching dresses, very similar in style to Autumn's wedding gown, in the exact sizes Jubilee and Elizabeth needed. The icing on the cake was that they were half off that day! That meant that although they had been $8.00, they were each only $4.00 that day!

When the kids brought them home they were so

giddy and so was I. Don't you love when kids walk in faith and see God provide in supernatural ways after having spent time praying for the answer? We nearly threw a party we were so excited. Just $4.00 each!! We still needed a dress for Ruby and it was fine with Autumn that it didn't match perfectly. Besides Ruby would be riding in her own little chariot.

Whenever we were out we would look around, but I wasn't sweating it. If the Lord had provided so miraculously for something as simple as Elizabeth and Jubilee, He surely had Ruby's dress covered as well.

Two days before leaving Arizona for Autumn's wedding in Colorado we went to a different local thrift store looking for a portable crib for our grandson Finn. As I walked by an end cap, there it was - a beautiful princess dress for Ruby, which was half off as well! It was only $4.32! We almost threw a party right there! The three flower girl dresses totaled $12.32 + tax and they were stunning! Our great God loves to provide in supernatural ways for everything – including the seemingly small stuff!

We could have rushed out and found flower girl dresses for upwards of $80.00 each, making the total over $200.00. Instead we prayed, we waited, we trusted and we watched and sure enough, in keeping with His miraculous nature, He provided three dresses, which were perfectly gorgeous, and totaled $12.32 plus tax! He is always faithful and He provides in miraculous ways.

We have a photo of the wedding in our Memorial Box with "$12.32 + tax" written on the back to always remind ourselves of His provision.

****

The three dresses for Autumn's wedding were not all He miraculously did for that special day! As we were getting ready to head to Autumn's wedding, we wondered what Ruby, as a flower girl, would ride down the aisle in - this was before she had her own wheelchair.

At first we reasoned a wagon might be best – as they were getting married beside a mountain lake. But then we realized that there would not be any room for a wagon in the car, not to mention that we actually didn't own one. We also realized it would be difficult to prop Ruby enough to endure the bumpy terrain to the altar.

We finally decided that a stroller would be best. However, as I thought about it, again, I wondered how we would ever bring our stroller along? Our van had only enough seats for all of us and Autumn's bridesmaid Molly, who was flying in to ride with us to Colorado. Of course we also needed to take a weeks worth of "stuff" and all the wedding clothing and gear. There was no-way-no-how that our bulky stroller would fit as well.

So I began to pray, "Lord would you provide a stroller in Colorado for the wedding?" I asked Autumn to ask some of her friends if we could borrow one. She asked but had been unable to find one. When we arrived in Colorado we still did not know where we were going to find a stroller. The day before the wedding I mentioned it to Vicki, Autumn's soon-to-be mother-in-law. She made a quick phone call and said, "I have a friend who can loan you her stroller." Whew! That was really close, Lord!

Now the thing that I didn't mention to anyone, well, except the Lord was this: "Lord, would you please be so gracious and have the stroller be something that doesn't clash with Ruby's dress? I know it could sound silly, but I know you care about the itsy-bitsy things that are concerning to me...so would you please?"

Somehow many think that they can only bring "the big stuff" to God. No, actually sweet friends, He says that He wants us "to cast all our cares upon Him, for He cares for us" (I Peter 5:7). And yes, I cared about the color of the stroller coordinating with Ruby's dress.

For instance, although I like the color orange, I just couldn't see Ruby looking all sweet and flower-girly in an orange stroller. Imagine an Army camo one for that matter! And although a black or brown stroller would be great – her gorgeous African face would just get lost. It was with all that in mind that I happened to mention to the Lord the stroller not clashing. No doubt about it, He cares about what I care about – even the seemingly small stuff!

So imagine my squealing, giggling and joyful glee when the borrowed stroller arrived – because what was Autumn's accent color? You got it! Hot pink! Ruby's dress was creamy white and her sash was hot pink! An absolutely perfect match!

Only our faithful God! He hears. He cares. He

works behind the scenes on our behalf long before we even whisper our cares to Him and then, in His all-magnificent way – He answers - even providing a borrowed stroller in the exact color of the bridesmaid's accent color!

There is no denying it friends. He is faithful. He cares about everything we care about! He longs to meet each of our needs – whether seemingly small or knowingly large. He has proven Himself trustworthy to me from the time I was a little girl. He wants you to completely trust Him too.

These sweet and simple stories will, Lord willing, jog your memory so that you, too, can be reminded of things He's done for you and remember how His hand has worked in your life over the years.

Often when we are walking through tough seasons, Dwight and I will turn to each other and say, "Remember when God did such-n-such?" and then retell a story from our **Memorial Box.** Each story encourages our souls, restores our faith and gives us great hope – He is working!

Chapter 14

Around the Corner

Here is one of my all-time favorite stories that occurred when we were pastoring in Virginia. (Yes, I realize I say that each story is one of my favorites but these stories are so crazy-good, because God doesn't ever do anything ho-hum. He just doesn't. He works wonders!! This story actually makes me giggle and throw up my hands to worship Him! He is just so amazing!)

We had just planted a church, which meant that times were lean. Very lean. With our equity from our home selling in Charlotte, North Carolina, we had built a sweet home on 24 acres. With six kids at the time; we really wanted to get a pool. Not a fancy pool, just a pool to splash around and cool off. So we started praying for one. We actually asked the Lord to provide a very specific pool. God's word reminds us in James 4:3, "You have not because you ask not."

Can you imagine if your son came to you and said, "Would you buy me a new shirt?" but didn't mention they actually wanted a white button shirt for their choir performance? You could run out and buy every color tee shirt, yet it wouldn't be what they needed (or even wanted). Then when you gave them the tee-shirt and they explained that it wouldn't work, you would likely question, "Why didn't you say so?"

Based on that scripture we had decided many years ago that when we were bringing our requests to the Lord we would ask specifically. So we asked for a pool that was shaped in an oval and was used but in great condition, so it would be very affordable.

At the time, there was a little newspaper in the Richmond and surrounding areas that came out each week and contained items being sold by individuals. So I began checking the paper. Before long I realized that that little paper covered many, many miles. Some places advertising could be hours away. So I changed my prayer – Lord, you know how busy Dwight is, could you please provide a used, oval above ground pool right here where we live for next to nothing?

Now if you knew how rural and little the town was that we were pastoring in, you would have laughed - Dwight did! Come on, what are the odds that a used, oval, above ground pool in great shape was anywhere nearby? The odds in the world's eyes were basically nil, but in God's eyes? (Big Smile inserted here.)

Before long we were leaving to go to Western New York for our family vacation. Just before leaving I saw an ad in that little paper. It was for a used, oval, above ground pool that had only been used one season. It was listed for sale for $700.00. And where was it listed? In our little *very* rural town!! I called the man and left a message, but didn't hear back. (This was back in the olden days, before cell phones.)

We left on our family vacation and while gone I thought about that pool and asked the Lord to hold it for us until we got back two weeks later. When we arrived back at home after our vacation, I found a message on our answering machine. A man's voice said, "Don't know if you are still interested, but my pool has not sold."

Dwight had already gone to the church office, so I called the man. He explained that he had just bought the house, the pool was in the backyard, he didn't want it and he had the receipt that the previous owner had paid about $5,000.00 for it the previous year! I told him I would call my husband, but just before he hung up he mentioned, "Listen, I really just want it out of here…I will sell it to you for $500.00" I was so excited since I despise negotiating! I hung up and called Dwight but in all my excitement I completely forgot to tell Dwight that he had lowered the price to $500.

Dwight called the man and was talking to him about the pool and planning when we could come to see it. They finished their conversation with Dwight asking, "How much was it again? I can't remember how much my wife said you are asking." He replied, "I started at $700 but really I just want it gone so I will sell it to you for $300."

Dwight knew how excited I was and called me immediately to tell me we were going to look at it the next day. He also told me the man had dropped the price to $300. I began whooping loudly! It started at $700., was just $500 moments before and in the time it took for me to tell Dwight and Dwight to call him back, he had dropped it *again* by $200 dollars!! I was laughing – come on dude, we aren't even there yet and you are dropping the price like a wild man!!

Oh, by the way, where did the guy live? Being our area was rural farmland – he lived five turns and a few miles from our little farmette! Oh yes he did! Dwight couldn't believe it. (Big smile inserted here!)

We went to look at it the next day. He wanted to show us the receipt. The previous owner had installed it the year before for over $5,000. It was an oval and it was wonderful!! Then the man said, "I really think you will need a new liner so I just don't feel comfortable selling it to you for $300, how about you just give me $200?" Unbelievable! For $200 we drove away with an almost brand-spankin' new pool which we didn't have to negotiate for and that we found almost literally around the corner from our very rural home.

Remember how Dwight had laughed at my prayer "that it would be in our neighborhood"? He was in awe of what God had done! Only God – He is so faithful!

That awesome pool brought us boatloads of fun for the years we pastored there and it reminded us daily that God is into the details – if we just ask! What needs do you specifically have? What concerns? What details are you asking for? God cares. God longs for you to talk with Him about it all.

In our Memorial Box sits an adorable little rubber duck that represents this story.

I will praise the name of God with song and magnify Him with thanksgiving.   Psalm 69:30

Chapter 15

$.09

    This is yet another one of my favorite "little" stories from around the same time that God provided the pool. He did something else that was seemingly small but enormous to me!

    As I finish up writing **The Memorial Box**, I have currently been homeschooling for 29 years. I didn't set out to homeschool that long – not at all! However, it has worked well and I have had the privilege of having each of our children home with me for their schooling years. Since all I ever wanted to do was be a mom, you can understand the thrill I have of spending each day with my favorite people.

    But years ago, during the season of pastoring in Virginia, I was homeschooling our five oldest: Abigail,

Tyler, Autumn, Emma and Graham. Each year we were in the routine of buying notebooks and supplies at the beginning of the school year when everything was on sale. But due to the lean financial season of planting a church, I had missed all the back-to-school sales and we were now well into the year and completely out of notebooks.

During this same season the Lord had been speaking to me about trusting Him, impressing on my heart that I was "not to worry about anything but instead I was to pray about everything" (Philippians 4:6,7).

Since I had wasted plenty of time as a worrier, based on the verse that we weren't to worry about anything, in this season, I was really working on removing *all* worry by meditating on "Do not worry about anything, instead pray about everything." (Philippians 4:6,7) So when I realized that we were out of notebooks, prior to this "get rid of all worry" season, my instant thoughts would have been: *Where am I going to find notebooks right now that I can afford? They never, ever have notebooks on sale at this time of year! How will we afford them? I need a bunch. Where should I go to look for them? How many would I need if I bought just the bare minimum to get us by?*

Most can probably relate to worry on some level. Worrying, fretting, trying to figure it all out, questioning

157

everything. My worrisome thoughts would have taken up precious time as they continued on and on, but I was learning to just share my need with the Lord and leave it with Him.

And I remember it like it was just yesterday. I was bending down to get something out of a lower cupboard in the kitchen and realizing I needed notebooks I simply whispered, "Lord, I need some notebooks. Actually I need lots of notebooks. Please provide them on sale where I can easily find them."

That was the end of my prayer. My mind went on to other things. I didn't worry. I didn't try to figure it out. I didn't even give the notebooks another thought.

Trust for me means not worrying - just giving it to Him and leaving it there. Trust literally puts the concern in the Lord's lap. And if I am really trusting, then I don't have to think another thing about it. He has it all figured out, He will take care of it and He will show up with the answer.

A few days later I went to Richmond to grocery shop and as I was walking into Wal-Mart, imagine my joy!! Right there, smack dab in front of me, at the very front entrance of the store, next to the greeter was an entire pallet of spiral notebooks: green, yellow, red, blue and black! They were the exact kind we use!

And are you ready for the very best part? They were only $.09 each! I would have thought it was a crazy out-of-the-box deal at $.25 each! But no! They were NINE CENTS!! Who would have guessed? I loaded our cart with piles and piles of notebooks and then bounced up the aisles rejoicing!! Nine cents each!

Having placed it on His lap and leaving it with Him, meant, no lost time, no anxious searching and absolutely no trying to figure it out. Which meant that our faithful, lavishly loving God met our very real seemingly small need in record time!!

Once upon a time we had an adorable little dollhouse-sized composition notebook in our Memorial Box but it was lost in the fire. One day we will find another.

"Therefore I tell you, do not be anxious about your life, what you will eat or what you will drink, nor about your body, what you will put on. Is not life more than food, and the body more than clothing? Look at the birds of the air: they neither sow nor reap nor gather into barns, and yet your heavenly Father feeds them. Are you not of more value than they? And which of you by being anxious can add a single hour to his span of life?"
Matthew 6:25-27

Chapter 16

70,000 Books

Dwight was about to begin his second year of law school the summer we were married. Two years later, Dwight finished law school, passed his bar exam and went to work for an attorney outside of Buffalo. After working for the attorney for almost a year, Dwight began to feel the Lord impressing on his heart that it would be a good idea to start his own private practice.

The thought of beginning a private practice would probably sound crazy to most experienced lawyers but Dwight felt confident that the Lord was clearly directing him. I was thrilled at the sound of the adventure! We began to pray that God would make a way and about the same time, Dwight began reading books about how to open your own law practice.

Strictly speaking from a human perspective, it sounded like an absurd idea! He was only 26 and I had just turned 22. In 1981, to think of such a thing at that age was crazy but actually, as we look back over our married life, we seem to really love living on the wild side of crazy.

While reading the many books about opening his own law practice, there was one common thread: *It's hard - really, really hard, it takes a lot of money and don't plan on taking any salary for a minimum of one full year.* Well we knew we could do the "it's really hard" part but the "it takes a lot of money" would probably be a problem if we didn't know the Lord and how faithful He had already been to provide for us!

The year before I had quit my job to be a stay-at-home-wife while we waited for the Lord to fill our empty arms. We depended solely on Dwight's income and so not having an income from Dwight meant that there would be zero. Again, not a problem for our giant God!!

We began to pray for provision. After all, if it was the Lord nudging Dwight to even think about it, He must have a really great plan for us to step out in faith and obedience. We would trust Him.

So we forged ahead.

One of the first things Dwight would need for his

law office was a desk. Again, we prayed, knowing that God had a good plan. We began to regularly check the classified ads and happened upon one that read: "Lawyer's cherry desk in excellent condition". We called and went to see it.

It turned out that the widow of an attorney was selling her husband's desk and was looking for someone who would love his beloved desk as much as he had loved it. The desk was everything Dwight had been dreaming of – a gorgeous cherry wood in pristine condition and if that wasn't wonderful enough – she was only asking $140 for it!! We were thrilled and joyfully thanked the Lord repeatedly for providing such a beautiful answer to our prayers! The elderly widow was equally tickled that a young attorney would be using it. Win/win in every way!

So with his desk ready for his use, we continued to pray that God would provide income that would get us through for as long as we needed. Boy did God ever have an amazing surprise for us!

One day, while working on cases and files at the law office where he was employed, Dwight came across a Catholic College in Atlanta that had purchased an entire library from another Catholic College that was closing near Albany, New York. The college in Atlanta that was purchasing the library was looking for a way to move all

162

70,000 books. Well that gave my hard-working husband an idea.

I will never forget his phone call that day as he shared with crazy-enthusiasm his idea: "Hey babe, what if we drove to Albany, NY and packed up the library, hired a semi and then I flew to meet the semi in Georgia to oversee the unloading? Seriously!! What if this is how God would provide our income for us to launch the law practice?"

I was giddy!! What an adventure!! We would make memories forever, "Hey remember the time we moved the 70,000 book library across the country?" I laugh now. We were so enthusiastic!

In the midst of the conversation though, I actually suggested that we wouldn't need a semi, because we could rent moving trucks and drive the library ourselves. Thankfully he was more realistic then I was and didn't entertain my ridiculously goofy idea!

He then went to his boss and asked if it would be okay if we bid on the job of moving the library. His boss said we were welcome to put in a bid as they were gathering bids from all over.

For several nights Dwight worked making calls, attempting to figure out exactly what it would take to pack up and move an entire library across the country and reassemble it in Georgia. Dwight was able to obtain several quotes from moving companies and semi-trucking companies to figure out what would be involved.

Since Dwight had actually worked packing law books for The Hein Law Book Company while in his early days of law school, he was familiar with the process of packing books! Finally he had a bid ready and he presented it to his boss as well as the college in Atlanta. Without any question, they said we had the job!! I will never forget the night we drove out of Buffalo with my brother Neil (who we had hired to help). We headed across New York State and stopped to pick up a friend of Neil's. I chuckle at our over-the-top joy the four of us had as we headed toward Albany, New York. We were embarking on a monumental-money-providing-mission and we couldn't wait!!

It turns out the college had actually already closed and had become a monastery somewhere along the way. It had an eerie silence everywhere we walked and was completely vacant save the library that was long since devoid of students.

A gentleman overseeing the former campus met Dwight briefly and told him, "By the way, they bought the shelves too. You will need to disassemble them as well and you will need to pack them in the truck too. Oh! And by the way, it all has to be out of here in 36 hours!"

Seriously, a camera should have been rolling with the expression on our faces with that news! What? All the shelves that were currently holding 70,000 books will have to go too? And it has to be done in 36 hours?

But we were good for our word and off to work we went. We worked through most of the first night. The second day we were full steam ahead, but were growing so weary.

Thankfully the Lord brought a semi-truck driver who saw the great task, took pity on us and eagerly helped us load the shelves. Our bodies were so exhausted, I can't even imagine what we would have done if Dwight had gone along with my unrealistic idea of driving it all to Atlanta ourselves. About a week later Dwight flew to Atlanta and to oversee the unloading of the books and shelves.

Sometimes I think of that library we moved some 35 years ago and wonder how many people miss out on amazing opportunities because they are afraid of hard work? Or perhaps some even think they are too important to do the hard stuff?

God definitely provided the books needing to be moved, we seized the opportunity and when it was all said and done He had provided income for about six months. What an amazingly faithful God!! And we have some wonderful out-of-the-box memories to boot!!

Before long Dwight gave his notice and we launched his practice! Remember how all the start-up books had the common thread that we would not to be able to take a salary for the first year? Well our lavishly providing God is so much bigger than any books about how to start a law practice. God grew Dwight's practice and the first year he brought home 1.5 times what he had made the previous year working for the other man!!

So friend, perhaps you are feeling nudged by the Lord to do something that will seem absurd to everyone around you. Maybe you know God is calling you to step out of your comfort zone. You might even have a burning desire to live radically for God, but the fear factor seems to be burning brighter. God will always provide for what He has called you to do. Always. He has never failed us, not even once.

In our Memorial Box we have two little books to remind us of God's provision through the library we moved!

And my God will supply every need of yours
according to his riches in glory in Christ Jesus.
Philippians 4:19

Chapter 17

Ezra

From the time I was a little girl I dreamed of having a rooster. Living in the city that wasn't reality.... but this girl sure could dream!

Then one Christmas, after moving to a picturesque 24 acres in the rolling countryside of Virginia, our oldest, Abigail surprised me with a huge box early one Christmas morning! Inside the box were two little roosters! I was beside myself with joy! That thoughtful girl of ours had heard over the years how I dreamed of having my own rooster and had searched for one just for me! Seriously, I giggled and smiled for months!

Not long after getting them, our neighbor's dog killed one. But the other one had survived the attack. The one that survived I had named Ezra after the Old

Testament prophet because every morning Ezra would *proclaim the favorable year of the Lord.*

Dwight was largely unimpressed and I do admit Ezra was a bit time-challenged. I told Dwight that he probably had ancestors in England because he would start his cock-a-doodle-dooing every morning around 2:30am.

Not kidding - every single night Ezra woke us and Dwight would mutter, "I'm gonna' kill that thing" to which I would reply, "Oh, isn't that the most beautiful sound in the entire world?" My poor husband just didn't appreciate the exquisite song of my sweet feathery friend.

During the day Ezra would come up on our big wrap around porch just to hang out with us. If he could have talked, I'm sure he would have said, "The family hangs out on the porch, I'm family, and so I'm sure they want me here too." And although Ezra was a bit time-challenged, he was extremely refined and never, not even once, did any of his backside business while he was on the porch visiting with us. Not sure how he pulled that off, other than that he really was a gentleman! Seriously. He was truly the answer to my lifelong dreams of having a rooster!

Having Multiple Sclerosis presented its challenges, so Dwight and I began to talk about the need to build a handicap accessible home. It would make it so much easier for me to maneuver. But moving also presented a potential concern. We would need to go to a rental after selling our home in order to use our equity to build our new home. So what in the world were we going to do with Ezra?

Our generous friend, Ralph, had offered his home as our rental once our home sold, but his rental was on one of the busiest roads in our town, not to mention, Ralph's rental home was very close to the road. I just didn't think Ezra would survive in that rental.

While pondering the Ezra dilemma, I also realized that it would be traumatic to move Ezra and try to get him to understand the whole moving thing and dangerous road thing. So I began to pray. Thankfully the Lord had been working on me about bringing every single care and concern to Him. Anytime I would think of Ezra I would mention it to the Lord. Specifically I asked if He would make a way for Ezra to just remain with our home. I even went so far as to ask the Lord to allow the people who would buy our home *to fall in love with our Ezra* so much so that they would be willing for him to stay.

I am very aware that not everyone has such a fascination for my feathery rooster friends. BUT God does care. He loves me enough to even care about my little time-challenged buddy, Ezra.

Months passed while we waited for the house to sell and after what seemed to be a trillion showings, one day my cell phone rang while checking out of the grocery store. I will never forget where I was standing when Almighty God did the miraculous for my little Ezra. The phone call went like this:

Our realtor: "Linny, this is Diana, we have an offer!!!"

Me: "Really? Oh Yippee Jesus!!! Is it a good offer?"

Diana: "Yeah, but it's really weird. The buyer's agent had to ask me something before he presented the offer. They are out-of-town buyers but before they even will present the offer they want to know if you would be willing to leave the rooster. The rooster came up to them on the front porch and they just fell in love with him and they don't even want to talk about the offer until they know that you are willing to leave your rooster. Seriously! That is the weirdest request I have EVER had. In all my years of real estate I have never had anyone want a rooster..."

Me (through shrieks of joy standing in the middle of the grocery store): "Oh God you are so good!! Diana, God's not only heard, He's answered my prayers!! I've been asking the Lord to allow the buyer to love and want Ezra and He did it Diana – He did it!" I then went on to tell her the whole story since only Dwight and the kids knew what my prayer had been!

Oh yes, dear friends, there is a sweet little rooster sitting in our **Memorial Box**. It is a constant reminder that God thoroughly cares about the "seemingly insignificant things" in our lives. He is the God of what would seem impossible or even silly to some!!

I mean really, what are the "odds" that someone would come to buy our home and want to be sure we were willing to leave Ezra? Only the God of the universe could stir the hearts of a family from out of state, which we had never met, to love my little Ezra, so much so that they would be prompted to make such a seemingly laughable request before they even presented the offer! What an amazing God we serve!

Any chance you have had something on your mind that seems ridiculous to talk to the Lord about? My Ezra would be a completely crazy concern to many, yet it was exactly what was on my mind! And since God's word tells us to bring all of our concerns to Him, I had to talk to Him about it. Don't ever be afraid to talk to the Lord about *anything*. He longs to hear from you about *everything*. Go for it. Really. He may just surprise you with an out-of-the-box response!

A little rooster (not nearly as dashing as my Ezra) sits in our Memorial Box to remind us of God's crazy provision for my dream-come-true feathery friend.

I will sing to the LORD as long as I live;
I will sing praise to my God while I have being.
Psalm 104:33

Chapter 18

The Contact Lens

Simultaneously while working on this book, the kids and I have been studying the life of Moses. The other day we came across a portion of scripture that I hadn't really remembered noticing before.

It's found in Exodus and confirms, again, why we are to have a **Memorial Box**. As we finished the verses, Isaiah, one of our two 13-year-old sons, looked up with joy and exclaimed, "Hey Mom!! You should talk about these verses in the book you are writing!"

This particular day we were studying Exodus 16 specifically, which is all about the Lord providing food in the form of manna for the Israelites to eat after they fled Egypt. Amazingly God provided the manna six days each week, without fail, for four hundred years!

Four hundred years!! Talk about Him being faithful - wow! He didn't forget to do it a few days here and there. He did it six days a week for four hundred years!!

What really caught our Isaiah's eye were the verses in Exodus 16:32-34:

Moses said, "This is what the LORD has commanded: 'Let an omer of it be kept throughout your generations, so that they may see the bread with which I fed you in the wilderness, when I brought you out of the land of Egypt.'" And Moses said to Aaron, "Take a jar, and put an omer of manna in it, and place it before the LORD to be kept throughout your generations." As the LORD commanded Moses, so Aaron placed it before the testimony to be kept.

This scripture is another clear example of God's desire for us to remember what He has done. The jar of manna would remind the Israelites of God's four hundred straight years of provision for them!

Our **Memorial Box** is overflowing with precious reminders of all God has done for us. Some of our stories go way back and this one is from my high school days, circa 1975. It really is one of my most favorite stories ever since it serves as a very powerful reminder of what our God can and will do – just because He loves us so!!

174

*"I will sing to the Lord, because
He has been so good to me!" Psalm 13:6*

Life growing up in my home was hard and after my dad lost his job things got even more complicated. He ruled our home with a strong arm and walking on eggshells was the safest idea. Since I had accepted Christ as a little girl all I wanted to do was please the Lord. I was an obedient, respectful daughter yet any stress or perceived stress in our home could throw family life into a tailspin without any effort.

It was my junior year of high school and I was dating our pastor's son. His family happened to be painting the outside of their home and I went over to help. We worked alongside his parents but they eventually went inside as he and I continued painting.

It was early spring and that meant it was extremely windy in Buffalo, New York. I was wearing hard contact lenses and my eyes were dry, probably from the wind, when suddenly one of my hard contact lenses was grabbed by the wind and blown right out of my eye!

My very first thought was, "Noooo!! Oh no!! My dad is going to kill me!!" Even though I had my own part-time job working in a nursing home and paid for all my own expenses (including a replacement contact) it wouldn't matter. I knew what would happen if my dad found out. That thought sent me into a panic!

I started to cry and at the same time I started to pray, out loud, and with passion!! "Jesus you know where that contact lens is! You know what is going to happen if my dad finds out! Please, Lord, please show me where that contact lens is! Please!"

I continued to plead with the Lord to show me where it was. From a human perspective, what are the odds of ever finding one little lone green hard contact lens blown away by the wind?? Yeah. Exactly. Not a chance!! I mean, for starters, think about it, there was *green* grass everywhere!! Really it looked useless to even try to look.

My boyfriend didn't know what to do. He was a kind-hearted, shy kind of guy but he just had that glazed look on his face. Of course with me crying, I'm pretty sure he was at a complete loss. The situation truly looked impossible!!

I started to look – first on my shirt!! Then he helped me look through my waist length brunette hair. Not finding it in my hair, we both stood and looked at the grass.

How in the world would we ever find a teeny, tiny green contact lens in a yard surrounded by green grass on this windy day? We looked at our paint pan, the paint can and our paint rollers. We checked my hair again. I rechecked my shirt and across my shoulders. It was so windy that from a human perspective this looked ridiculously hopeless.

But even at my young age of 16, I already had a crazy-confidence that my God could do anything!! I reasoned, if He could part the flood-level swollen Jordan River for the Israelites to walk through on *dry* ground, if He could give sight to a blind man, if He could feed a crowd larger than 5,000 with two small loaves and five fish, if He could close the mouths of the hungry lions while Daniel spent the night in their den, if He could allow three obedient men to hang out without even being slightly burned in a fiery furnace that was heated up seven times hotter than normal and if He could use one jar of oil to fill an enormous number of empty jars from that same one jar of oil for a widow and her son...*then finding my tiny fly-away contact lens definitely was not too big of a task for my loving Heavenly Father!*

So I got down on my knees and started looking through the blades of grass and I continued to pray aloud. My boyfriend got down and started looking too. Of course, I knew that there was also the possibility that one of us had stepped on it, but I asked the Lord to pull it out and make it whole...just please Lord, return my contact lens back to me!

He and I continued searching for probably about 45 minutes. Slowly, carefully, moving aside each blade of grass, inch by inch. We found nothing. And for the record, I was not going to give up. (In hind sight, I'm also guessing my boyfriend thought I was nuts.) It really, really, really did look impossible. The same wind that had whipped it out of my eye to begin with was still blowing, so just how far could it have gone?? It could be anywhere!!

Yet I totally and completely believed that He was going to show me exactly where it was and I was not going to give up until He did! If it had blown 500 feet away, He was more than capable of having a ministering angel pick that little lens up and put it where I could find it!!

We continued looking as I pleaded, "Show me Lord exactly where it is!" Probably an hour had passed and all of a sudden I felt the Lord whisper to me, "Stand up!" So I stood up. Then I waited. Again, I felt Him whisper with His still small voice, "Walk over there, I will tell you when to stop." My boyfriend had stopped looking and was watching me as I silently walked, slowly, gingerly toward where I felt He had said to go. Bit by bit I inched along, lightly taking each step.

Now standing approximately 12 feet from where we had been painting and looking, I felt Him say, "Bend down and part the grass!" I bent down, and in one exacting movement, I literally parted the grass and probably *two inches down*, tucked among thousands of blades of grass, was my green-tinted, hard contact lens!!!!

Crying while typing more than 40 years later I can still feel the overwhelming hysteria as I grabbed that contact lens and started screaming, jumping up and down, while rejoicing at what God had done!!

I ran to my boyfriend, "LOOK! LOOK!! Do you see what God has done? Did you see where it was?? DID YOU SEE? God told me exactly where to look. God showed me where it was! Did you see that??" My exuberance was unmatched!!

My loving Heavenly Father understood completely what would be in store if I had gone home without that contact and He had *miraculously* answered my prayer!! He had spoken so precisely and He had done it in such a dramatic way!! He had shown me where it was, many, many feet from where it had all started. It was an amazing time of faith building for me. It also encouraged me, again, how to recognize and hear His voice.

The other thing that struck me that day was that He *had not done it instantly*. I couldn't help but wonder and think that the reason for the length of

179

searching was that He had wanted to see if I would persevere in my trust of Him. What if I had looked at the situation and said it was impossible? After all it legitimately looked impossible! What if I had only looked for a little bit and given up? The hour that we searched, against all human odds, He had been building my faith and I really do believe He was testing my faith as well. He was building my faith to a point of complete trust that He was going to direct me to exactly where it was. What if I had quit? What if I had stopped looking after a few minutes? What if I had decided after a half hour that that was enough? What if I had just given up and never looked at all because it looked impossible?

So now, let me ask…are there some things that you are about to give up on? Are there situations that look impossible? If there a specific situation that you think is just too big humanly speaking, then your situation is perfect for God!! Because our God is way bigger than any impossible circumstance!!! In fact, He is more than able for you situation. Do you know that you are actually on His mind right now?

I learned a valuable lesson that day and it is contained in this verse: *And without faith it is impossible to please God, because anyone who comes to Him must believe that He exists and that He rewards those who earnestly seek Him. Hebrews 11:6* My faith was clinging to the fact that

180

God does the impossible, while remembering that I had
already seen God do the miraculous, giving me the
ability to stand firm and wait for Him to move again.

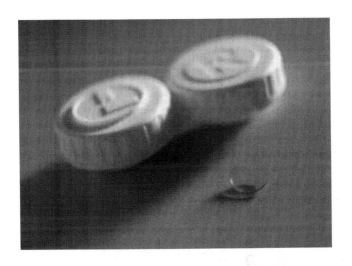

In our Memorial Box we have

a little contact lens case

to remind us of the day

God met me in a very real way!!

Answer me when I call to you,
my righteous God.
Give me relief from my distress;
have mercy on me and hear my prayer.
Psalm 4:1

Chapter 19

"Pick It Up!"

This is one of the stories where we stand and marvel at the highly detailed and powerfully intricate moving of Almighty God.

It was May of 2006 when we went as a family to our denomination's convention in DC – the very same convention that we found the adoption agency for our Isaiah! Washington, DC is one of our favorite cities and we were thrilled to be spending free time in our nation's capital. One of the afternoons we decided to take the kids to the Smithsonian Air and Space Museum. Dwight and I had taken our older kids many years before and we thought the younger ones would enjoy it now as well.

As the afternoon wore on, everyone was getting tired and we knew we would need to get back for a quick rest before the evening session started. Dwight headed toward the doors to lead us out of the building and I thought, "Why is he taking us out the opposite side of the building from where we came in?" It was odd. In my head I was thinking, "Walking out this side will give us an even further walk back to the hotel!!"

As Dwight exited, he turned back over his shoulder and called to us, "I'm going to hail a cab for all of us." Okay, good. I was so glad! The kids and I began heading toward the outdoor stairs. The MS had really been acting up, so I was slow going as we headed down the many stairs on the backside of the Air and Space building.

As I glanced up to watch Dwight, I saw that there was a cab right in front of where we had exited. But instead of going to that cab, he was actually running a couple of hundred feet down to where a cab had just pulled up! I stood there for a second wondering what in the world he was doing. Why had he not gone to the cab that was closer?

Truthfully I was getting a tad annoyed. Walking had become a chore (because of the MS) and here he was going to a cab that was even further away. As he was heading toward that cab I noticed people were getting out of it but I was still in the middle of all the stairs so although I glanced a few times, I didn't really take in any details.

By now Dwight had turned around and motioned for us to "come on" because the cabbie (at the cab which was further away) had agreed to take us.

As we reached the cab, Dwight was telling Emma, Graham and Liberty to get in the back. I was the last one to the cab and while watching the kids climb in, I glanced down and saw something in the road. It was right next to the curb, but in the road.

I noticed it was a pocket calendar, the rectangular kind, with the little plastic cover. As I moved to get into the cab, I turned to Dennis (our friend who was with us) and quipped, "Oh look, someone's going to be bummed, they dropped their pocket calendar."

The kids were climbing in when suddenly I felt compelled to pick it up. Then I thought, "Like I'm going to try to find whoever owns it and return it to them. Nah. They really won't miss it all that much."

It was then that I literally went to put my foot in the cab and I heard the Lord whisper firmly, **"Pick it up!"** So I stepped back and reaching down, I picked it up. Turning quickly I pulled my right leg into the cab and we were off! It was crowded in the cab and Liberty shuffled over onto my lap.

Dwight was talking to the driver up front as I gave a quick peek into the calendar to see if I could figure out whose it was to return it. The place inside the cover where the owner's name would normally be written did indeed have a name. The only problem was that it was written in an Asian language! Oh brother - that wasn't a lot of help to return it to the rightful owner! I turned the pages. They were filled with writing. But nothing was really in English. Then I noticed in the little plastic inside flap a small envelope. I pulled it out as we were driving down the highway and opened it up. I gasped!

There was money - lots of money! There were many one hundred dollar bills and there was also a check. I am sure that my eyes were popping out of my head. Astonished I said, "This thing is full of money."

Dwight turned around and stared at me. "Are you serious?" he asked as I started counting. Between the cash and the check there was almost $3,000.! I could not believe my eyes!

When I took a closer look at the check, it had the name of a church on it, meaning a church had given this check to someone and I realized that the name on the check was likely the owner of the calendar.

Silly as it might sound, I have always dreamed of being a detective and over the years I've done my share of "detective work". When I saw that the check had been given from a church, and the name of the person it was written to was an Asian name I started praying.

"Lord you have to help me find this person!"

Funny how one minute I'm feeling grumpy about having to walk to the faraway cabbie and now suddenly I'm so excited that I am holding this little mystery calendar that was full of money. I was so thrilled, in fact, that I could hardly stand it!

We got back to the hotel and I tried to search and find information about the church. Nothing came up. Then I tried White Pages. Nothing. There was actually an accounting firm's name from the west coast also on the check. I decided to search for that. My family went to get something to eat as I worked fervently to find out whose calendar I had found.

Eventually I found a number that seemed to be associated with the accounting firm. Dialing it, I heard a young woman answer. Her sweet accent made me guess that she was also Asian. I asked if she had a minute while I explained this long, weird story. I even mentioned that we were on the East coast because we were attending a Pastor's convention. She listened but did not ask any questions nor did she offer any words at all, but said, "Let me call you back" and took down my phone number.

As I waited I began to feel real concern for the person who had lost the pocket calendar. I prayed that God would give them peace and that this calendar and envelope full of money would be returned to them quickly. After what seemed like an eternity, my cell phone rang. A woman, who spoke basically zero English was on the other end. I tried explaining to her what was going on, but she was unable to understand. She hung up. Eventually someone who spoke more fluent English called me. And the story began to unfold.

Are you ready for this?

The owner of the calendar and its contents was a pastor from a country that does not allow the gospel to be preached. He had flown to Washington, DC to attend our very own denomination's convention - the same convention we were attending!! He was not a pastor in our denomination, but had been invited to come because of his involvement in the underground church in his country.

He was a very well respected and an extremely influential man in his country – having been imprisoned for his faith and work for the gospel of Jesus Christ. I can hardly type about him without crying.

This great man of God, brave and courageous in his country, had come to the United States to tell of the plight of the underground church! He was traveling and sharing the stories of his country with people across the United States. Encouraged by his bravery, they had been giving him monetary donations to support the work of the underground churches in his country. The pile of money was from all his speaking engagements!

Some American friends had taken him to tour the Smithsonian. Remember how Dwight had gone to that faraway cab? This brave pastor was one of the people who had just gotten out of the very cab we had climbed into. As he ventured out of the cab he had somehow dropped his pocket calendar!

He had not discovered immediately that it was missing but when he did – he was frantic! He had absolutely no idea where he could have lost it. But God knew and had been protecting it until we climbed into the same cab! We climbed in probably within less than one minute of it being dropped on the street!!

When this precious man discovered it missing, he told the people he was with and they immediately joined together and started to pray, "God please will YOU protect this calendar and the money inside it and return it to him?" They said that in the natural it was a long shot, BUT in the supernatural they knew that we have a very powerful, all-knowing, miraculous God!

Yes, faithful God. Our miracle-working, mountain-moving, awe-inspiring, GASP-giving God had not allowed that envelope to rest in that street for anything more than a minute - just long enough for us to get down to the street!

If that wasn't amazing enough, when we were arranging the return of the calendar and money, it turns out that the man was not just staying at our same hotel – he was on the exact same floor we were on! He and I actually rode the elevator down together! He didn't speak English and of course, I had no idea who I was looking for as I went down to the lobby. Can you really imagine all the details that went into that being orchestrated by God? I had the privilege of hugging this Great Man of God. He was weeping. He was so grateful and kept crying and crying. I was crying too. Dwight has a picture of me giving it to him and I am so grateful.

And yes, I was so ashamed that I had been aggravated at Dwight for going to the back side of the Smithsonian with all the stairs as well as that faraway cab! Just think, God was directing my man of God's steps so I could scoop up that calendar and have the privilege of helping a brave pastor!

Many lessons were learned that day including the reality that if we submit to our God on a daily basis and ask Him to use us, He will!! How God loves His children and how He maneuvers events and circumstances to provide for His own!! Imagine if I had not obeyed the whispers, I would have missed an incredible privilege as the story unfolded!

Don't misunderstand - I believe God would have

used someone else to bring the money safely back to the great man of God had I not obeyed His whispers. But this time, He used me. However, it reinforced in my heart, that we must all be willing listeners and doers when He whispers, as His whispers will sometimes lead to extraordinary divine appointments that only He could orchestrate.

A similar pocket calendar is in our Memorial Box to remind us of the great man of God who we had the privilege of meeting one day in Washington, DC.

When we think of the story of this brave man of God, we are reminded to pray for the persecuted church around the world as found in Hebrews 13:3

"Continue to remember those in prison as if you were together with them in prison, and those who are mistreated as if you yourselves were suffering." May God give strength, peace and comfort to those in prison for Christ and may they see God's miraculous hand at work in their lives in spite of their suffering.

Chapter 20

A Final Story

As I began typing *The Memorial Box* I prayed daily about what I would share as the final story. I longed for the last story to be personal, unquestionably powerful while emphatically declaring the undeniable faithfulness of our magnificent God.

All along I've had one prayer and only one prayer while writing this book. My deepest desire is that God would use *The Memorial Box* to open each individual's heart to not only the magnitude of God's love for them, but also the compelling truth that they were created by the God of the Universe for a simple, yet very personal relationship with Him. Because of His great love for His kids, He is always at work around them on their behalf.

As the months passed writing, I continued to pray

asking the Lord what the final story should be. He kept the answer to Himself and I'm glad He did - because little did I know that I was about to walk an unexpected, very personal journey that would become the final story.

It is really remarkable sweet friends. Just eight weeks ago, as I lay in the hospital unsure of my future, I had incredible peace.

Over and over throughout each day, The Lord would bring our **Memorial Box** stories to my mind. Each story served to remind me just how faithful He had been in the past! Remembering His faithfulness in the past brought enormous comfort while also bringing peaceful assurance the He was not about to leave me high and dry on the 5th floor of a large Phoenix Hospital. He would be my "ever present help in time of need." (Psalm 46:1)

And so the story unfolds…

Our fourth oldest, Emma, moved to Africa as a single 19-year-old. She had been talking almost daily, from the age of six and a half, about moving to care for the orphans! Because of her relentless passion for the orphan, Dwight first took her to Africa when she was just 14-years-old.

In the following years, either Dwight or I along with Emma would co-lead mission teams to Africa preparing her in the best way we knew how to live there on her own. Daddy was the one who flew with her on her twelfth trip to Africa as she permanently moved at 19-years-old.

Her heart burdened for special needs orphans in particular; Emma quickly began the necessary paperwork to found a home for orphans with severe needs. The city of 3 million where God directed her to live did not have a home for special needs orphans. (The website of her home: TheGemFoundation.com) Currently The Gem has 31 precious Gems who call it home. There are also 45 employees that serve in various capacities.

The year before Emma moved to Africa Dwight and I founded a nonprofit. Our ministry, *International Voice of the Orphan* (IVO), is multi-faceted but we have one desire: To care for orphans and challenge others to help in one-way or another!

Each month our ministry, IVO, serves 16,000 meals to orphans in India, Sri Lanka, West Africa and Uganda; we lead mission teams to serve the orphan four times a year; fund severe medical needs of orphans and vulnerable children; as well as overseeing fundraising for *The Gem Foundation*.

Dwight and I make at least four trips each year to visit Emma, Josh, their son and The Gems. While one goes, the other is at home caring for our nine treasures

we still have at home. We love *The Gem Foundation* and
we love Africa! I've always said, "If there were two of
me, one would live in Africa where I could serve at The
Gem as well!"

So a few months ago, in March 2017, I traveled alone
to spend some time with Emma, Josh, their son and their
Gems. After enjoying eleven days with Emma and her
crew, I flew the 27 hours toward home. As I flew across
the continents I was able to continue writing **The
Memorial Box**.

Arriving home I felt awesome!! I swung into gear
caring for our nine kids still at home. Two days later
though, I was changing our 4-year-old's crib sheet and
while leaning over the side rail and pressing the mattress
into the corner of the crib I heard an audible "POP!"
from my right lower ribs. The pain was so excruciating
it actually knocked the wind out of me and I was left
gasping for breath!

Our 11-year-old Elizabeth had been in the laundry
room at the time and came immediately to see what was
going on - she couldn't tell if I was laughing or crying
loudly! Since I've fractured a rib on my lower right side
in the past, I could only guess it likely was fractured
again. It hurt like crazy, was tender and made picking
up Birdie and Ruby impossible. I was so annoyed with
myself! How could I do this again?

A few days later our third oldest, Autumn, flew to Phoenix for a visit with her two little ones. I was thrilled to have her home for some fun!

Unfortunately two days after her arrival I began to feel sick. I went to bed early and thought it must be the jet lag finally catching up with me. Yet each day of Autumn's ten day visit, I continued to grow sicker. I was forcing myself to drink a little water in an effort to remain hydrated. Autumn and her two babies flew home. Although I wanted to play, I had just been too sick.

My body was clearly fighting something and I was beginning to grow concerned. I was now running a fever, which was hovering around 101.6.

On Sunday, April 30th Emma texted me from Africa, *"Mom! You have to get to a doctor! Go to the ER! If I was sick this long you would be so mad at me for not going to the doctor to figure it out. You would have also texted Josh and told him he better take me to the doctor or else!"*

Her text made me smile. True enough, I had now been sick for about 2.5 weeks. I would have not been happy if she had been sick, sleeping day and night and now running a fever and had not gone after 2.5 weeks to figure out what was wrong!

The following day I decided I would force myself to take a shower and then go to the family room to have____ worship and Bible study with the kids before school. Maybe if I would just get up and do it, I would begin to feel better!

When I finished dressing, I headed toward the bedroom door but didn't have the strength to leave our room. I remember slumping over the bed in a heap. My body just couldn't do it.

A few minutes later Dwight came and found me stretched across the bed at an angle. I wasn't unconscious but I was struggling to wake up so he helped me into bed.

I slept all day. At one point Dwight told me that my friend Missy was going to bring dinner to our family. Her husband Doug, who is on staff at the church we attend, was coming with her. I wondered if Doug would be willing to anoint me with oil according to James 5:14-16.

Before dinnertime Missy and Doug arrived. My sweet friend came into my bedroom and sat down on the side of my bed as we talked. Missy mentioned that her brother had had Valley Fever and she was wondering if maybe that's what this was. I definitely had several of the symptoms and it can be very serious for people who have autoimmune disorders. Since I have four that concerned us both.

Eventually Doug came in to anoint me with oil. Dwight gathered the kids together around our bed as Doug prayed over me. It was a beautiful time together. I opened my eyes when Doug finished praying and looked at my pile of treasures gathered around. My heart was smiling big as I thought, "I'm living my dream. I have definitely been blessed far more than I've ever deserved!"

After dinner Dwight and I agreed that he should take me to the Emergency Room. That trip is another story for another day, but suffice it to say the ER staff was in a tizzy because I had been to Africa recently. They were thinking Ebola and I was thinking they were nuts. I tried to explain that there had not been a single case of Ebola since 2012 in the country that I had been to, not to mention that I really didn't have any of the symptoms.

They ran some tests while I slept between each one. At one point they said I had markers indicating a heart attack was likely in the next few days. (What?) Then they said they thought I might have blood clots in my lungs. (Are you serious?) They then decided that they were going to transfer me to a larger hospital. At 2:30am the ER doc came in and announced abruptly, "You must have a virus. If you aren't better in a few days you need to go and be tested for Valley Fever. You can go home." WHAT?

While in the ER Dwight had been texting Liberty, our five married kids and their spouses, keeping them all up to date in our family chat. Once we reached home Emma texted, "Daddy, you will take her to a different hospital in the morning, right?"

Emma was going to be relentless. In hindsight, she was right. I was too sick to not figure this out. The upside of the abrupt discharge was that I got to go back and climb in my own bed. But the whole experience at that ER had left us with a sour taste.

Tuesday morning Emma texted me, "Mom, if you don't go find a different hospital I will shut my phone off." I had to smile. This is the same determination that moved her to Africa at 19-years-old, alone and single! I ignored her adamant demand and tried to text about something light-hearted. She would not answer me. Ugh!! I gave up and said I would figure out what hospital to go to by the next day.

That seemed to slightly appease her. A few hours later, as she was heading to bed on the other side of the world she made one more plea, "Mom we need you! Go to another hospital!" Her words pierced my heart. I hadn't really thought this could be life threatening in any way. But it's true I have nine precious treasures that I care for day in and day out. Two of them are considered quadriplegics. Three of our treasures are what we call "lifers"…we get to keep them for their entire lives! Two of our treasures are medically fragile…each day with them is a gift!

So with Emma's words echoing in my heart all day, I knew I had to do something, but what?

Unbeknownst to me Graham, our fifth oldest, had called Dwight after dinner. Graham told him, "Mom needs to go tonight to the best hospital in Phoenix."

Dwight replied, "Do you know your mother? She is so stubborn! She already went to an ER last night. There is no way she will be willing to go back tonight." Graham told him to tell me that he would drive me.

Having just used the ladies room I was returning to bed when Dwight walked in, "Graham wants you to go back to another hospital tonight, he and Savannah will take you." Fully expecting me to tell him I wasn't interested, Dwight spun his head toward me in shock as I responded, "If he's willing to take me, I will go."

I had quickly agreed for two reasons: One was because I no longer wanted to stay awake and my fever was still there. The other reason was because Graham had offered to drive.

The previous night we had arrived home from the ER after 2:30am and Dwight was exhausted. I knew that a second night of driving and then sitting into the night would take a lot out of him. He works very long, hard hours and I didn't want to put his health at risk with little sleep. So with Graham's offer, I knew it was time.

Before long Graham and Savannah were driving me to the most respected hospital in downtown Phoenix. Little did we know that this would be a lifesaver move!

As we were walking through the ER doors that night the Lord whispered to me part of Lauren Daigle's song "Trust in You".

You are my strength and comfort
You are my steady hand
You are my firm foundation
The rock on which I stand
Your ways are always higher
Your plans are always good
There's not a place where I'll go
You've not already stood

This song had been part of our daily worship for months. The two lines in particular that I had been meditating on since first hearing it: ***"There's not a place where I'll go you've not already stood."***

The powerful Biblical truth that we will never face anything where God had not only gone before us, but He has actually stood, had pierced my soul and I had been meditating on those words for months.

Scripture tells that that He goes before us but somehow I had only pictured Him passing through briefly where we are headed orchestrating details.

But somehow those powerful lines, "There's not a place where I'll go that you've not already *stood*" touched an even deeper place in my being.

Over the last few months I had begun to picture Jesus standing, firmly planted, and looking about from every possible vantage point to see what we would need with precision detail.

I firmly believe that there is nothing in our lives that is given to chance. Our God is a God of magnificent detail! Just look at the intricacies of the more than 400,000 species of flowering plants!! There is zero possibility that He throws everything to happenstance! He carefully orchestrates every single facet of our lives.

So as Savannah, Graham and I entered the ER that night, I realized that our great and powerful God had stood inside the massive doors and looked about, from every single vantage point and weighed the situation. "Linny will need this doctor, that room, this nurse and technician" and so on as He prepared the entire journey. Every piece of the puzzle, He already knew. The only thing I needed to do was trust Him.

Skeptics might say, "Well then what happened the previous night at the other ER? Where was God then?"

Friends, He was there! He was orchestrating the details so that they would show incompetence and I would end up, the next night, at the best possible hospital for my very serious problem.

Once inside the Emergency Department we noticed many, many waiting their turn ahead of us. No doubt, it looked like this would be a long wait.

However, with no explanation to this moment, we never even sat down! For some reason the triage staff saw me and immediately led us into a room where a tall handsome ER doctor would come in promptly. He was probably in his early 40s and was so very kind! In fact, as God's grace would have it, when he heard that I had just returned from Africa he smiled big and explained, "My family and I have just returned from serving in Kenya!" Wow Lord!! A doctor who wasn't freaked out that I had just been in Africa!!

While he began asking me questions I pulled out all the paperwork from the other hospital's ER visit the previous night. Handing it to him I explained that they had sent me home saying I should be checked for Valley Fever if I wasn't well in a few days.

He stepped out of the room to have copies made and stepping back in he questioned hesitantly, "Is it all right with you if we just start completely over?" When he posed that question, I felt relief! Since the not-so-fun trip to the other ER the previous night had been a gigantic waste of time, why not start at the very beginning?

He asked me about everything he could think of. I even mentioned to him how I had popped my ribs changing Birdie's crib sheet a few weeks back and how much they were still hurting. It didn't seem relevant, but he really did ask about everything!

Within a couple of minutes we were taken into a room where I settled onto an ER bed. Soon a jovial technician came in to draw blood. He joked with the three of us as he took six vials and then two bottles that looked like they each held about 6 oz. I had never seen anything like it!

It was sweet to have Graham and Savannah with me. They are an amazing team together – wise beyond their years, passionate about sharing the good news of Jesus and so much fun! Although I was sleepy, we talked about many things.

About an hour later the ER doctor returned. He looked concerned as he questioned me, "Can you tell me again about your rib injury?" That wasn't on my radar at all, but, again, I explained how I been changing Birdie's sheet, was leaning over with my full weight on the crib rail and I had heard a loud POP!

When I finished I asked, "Do you think I've been so sick from that injury?" He had a very serious expression as he responded, *"Your liver is very sick* and I'm wondering if your liver was already sick, but the injury was the catalyst for your liver to become even sicker."

Wait! What did he say? My mind was now swirling! My liver was very sick? Here I was thinking I probably had Valley Fever and he was saying that my liver was very sick! My liver? Wait! I need my liver!

He continued, "Are you one of those people who take Tylenol all the time?" Surprised by his question I stammered, "Oh no! No! I take it about once a year, only if I am in agony! I hate all medications!"

After he left my room I lay quietly thinking and praying, "Lord please use my time in the hospital to draw people to you. Use me in whatever way you want. With each person who enters my room, please let them see Jesus in me. Let my room be a place of peace for all who enter."

Before long my nurse came in to tell me I would be going for a sonogram in a few minutes. Graham was getting sleepy and had to work early in the morning and it was decided that he would head home for some sleep. I told them both to go but Savannah insisted that she would stay with me.

After the sonogram, I came back to the room. We both were sleepy but the room happened to be beside a set of doors that accessed the entire main hospital and this huge hospital had people coming and going. We would just start to doze and the doors would jolt us awake.

About an hour after Graham left, the ER doctor came in again. He got right to the point, "We are trying very hard to figure out why your liver is so sick. For a woman your age your ALT should be below 40, however, yours is over 4,000 and your AST should be below 20 but yours is right at 4,000"… and his voice trailed off.

Savannah was seated behind and off to the side of him, so while he was talking my eyes were darting back and forth between him and zeroing in on her expression as he talked. Our sweet daughter-in-love, Savannah, has one semester left of nursing school and is at the top of her class! I knew she would have a better understanding of all he was saying, because I definitely had no clue!

But as I peered at her precious face, I could not tell anything. She was listening intently, but nothing else.

When he began to announce all the numbers, I reasoned, "Okay, well maybe liver numbers can go to 30,000 so mine aren't necessarily that bad…" and being someone who often resorts to comic relief when things seem to be getting scary, I quipped, "So do I win something with numbers like that?" He ignored me completely. I gulped. This must be really serious!

He told me that I would be having more tests because they needed to figure out what had caused my liver to get so sick. Before long I was taken for an echocardiogram, chest X-rays, a CT scan, another sonogram and a few other tests.

About 4:30am I was up on one of the floors being wheeled back to the ER after having a second sonogram done. I was having a pleasant conversation with the young man who was transporting me. With no warning, two men in white coats stopped my cart and questioned, "Mrs. Saunders?" Surprised I answered, "Uh, yes." "We are your surgeons and we need to talk to you!"

My eyes grew wide and my heart rate picked up a bit as I tried to wrap my head around what he had just said. No one had said anything about surgery! What kind of surgery would they even do?

Quickly looking around he saw an open room down the hall, "Here! We'll go down this hall and in this curtained room!" As the two surgeons led the way, I questioned, "Am I going to surgery?" The surgeon who was about my age answered, "I'm not sure yet. We just need to talk."

I was so confused and definitely a little scared!! It was the middle of the night and I was on some random floor being transported between my ER room and a sonogram. Now, two surgeons had hunted me down to talk to me? What was really going on?

The older surgeon began with a battery of questions but not before asking if he knew me because I looked so familiar. I couldn't imagine how I might know him but I asked him if maybe we attended the same church. He wondered what church I went to. I told him but he shook his head that that wasn't it. He then proceeded to ask me everything under the sun!

In the midst of his questions, he also wondered if I was a regular Tylenol-popper? Wrinkling my nose, I quietly explained that I actually stay away from meds, if possible! I also mentioned that I really believe that God made our bodies remarkably well and that often it just takes a little time for them to heal on their own. He wanted to know about my lifestyle, how I spend my days and my recent trip to Africa.

I loved telling him that I was a mom to 14 treasures with nine still at home. Of course I told him that of the 14, eleven were adopted from around the world. I even joked a bit about Dwight and I thinking that with only nine left at home we consider ourselves "empty nesting"! Since he was about my age, he laughed heartily.

I shared a speck about our ministry and our love for the orphan, also about frequently traveling to Africa because of both our ministry and Emma's. He explained that although he didn't think surgery would be needed at this moment my liver was very sick so we would wait and see.

On a comical note, he also asked me if I was one of "those people" who are into "weird healing stuff"? That made me smile. I questioned what he meant by "weird healing stuff". He responded, "You know, one of those people who does cleanses and stuff." I smiled and said that I had done a few cleanses in my life.

As he turned to leave, he grasped my ankle and gently shook it and smiling, he sweetly said, "You're pretty cool and I like you a lot!"

After the two surgeons left, I lay waiting a long time for another transport person to come get me to return me to my ER room. I waited for probably an hour and while I was waiting, Dwight had gotten up and was texting me. I told him what I knew so far: "It's my liver. It's very sick. I've had so many tests I've lost track. Two surgeons just hunted me down to talk to me. I'm feeling concerned." He told me he couldn't sleep and would be at the hospital soon.

Eventually I was returned to my ER room. Poor Savannah had been waiting all that time and had a test in the morning! She had not slept all night so I told her she needed to go home. Before long Graham came and picked her up. Dwight arrived as the sun was just beginning to come up. It felt so good to have my best friend by my side.

After Dwight arrived a team of Internists came in to see me. They, of course, asked me a zillion questions. While they were there in my room, a doctor brought the news that I had Acute Hepatitis A. I was stunned! Seriously? Acute Hepatitis A? I had never even thought of that! Since Dwight had had Hepatitis A (which I wrote about in the first chapter of this book) I was familiar with it, yet it had never even crossed any of our minds since my symptoms were so different!

But, after telling us that it was Acute Hepatitis A, they went on to say that my liver was not responding in a way that was consistent with Hepatitis A. My liver was actually in critical condition with both my ALT and AST numbers perilously out of control!

In the early morning hours, the Liver Transplant Specialist arrived and Dwight had stepped out in the hall to talk with her. I could see the concern on his face from where I lay talking to my friend Missy who had now also arrived.

Missy had brought me a beautiful cross to cling to. It was specially carved to wrap in a person's fist as they cling to it. The creator of the cross writes in an accompanying pamphlet that although there is absolutely no power in the little cross, it was created to remind each person who they are actually clinging to – Jesus!! It now sits beside my bed as a daily reminder of God's overwhelming faithfulness to me.

Missy was very teary-eyed that morning as we talked about what was going on with my liver. I had told her my AST and ALT numbers in the night when she was texting to check on me.

Through tears she told me that if I needed a liver transplant she was going to be tested and would share her liver with me. She also mentioned that Doug would be tested too. I was so humbled that they would love me enough to be willing to share their liver with me but I was also kind of confused.

No one had said anything about possibly needing a liver transplant and I could not even fathom the thought that I might need one. No doubt, I did not understand what exactly the skyrocket numbers meant and obviously those closest to me were doing some investigating and figuring it all out on their own!!

Dwight and Dr. B, the Liver Transplant Specialist, talked for a long time in the hallway. Eventually they both joined us in my room where we were talking about nothing special when a beautiful young black woman entered my ER room to draw more blood. She was so sweet, all smiles, as she reached to check my veins. As she leaned over me, her nametag became visible to Missy who was seated beside me.

Under her breath Missy whispered, "Did you see her name?" I shook my head no and Missy whispered, "Ruby!" Oh my!! Since our second youngest daughter is Ruby, I was so excited! I love the name Ruby and had not met many other Rubys!

As this beautiful Ruby stepped back to get her supplies I joyfully exclaimed, "Oh my gracious!! You are Ruby? I have a Ruby!!" Pausing, I continued, "In fact she is every bit as beautiful as you!"

As I said that, I saw her face wrinkle *ever so slightly*. Noticing her facial expression change for a split second I teasingly questioned, "Wait! You don't think I could have a daughter as beautiful as you, do you?"

Laughing heartily now I continued, "Oh Ruby! You don't, do you? You are thinking, 'There is no way a white girl could be as beautiful as me!' Isn't that what you are thinking? Come on! I busted you, didn't I? Well you just have to see my daughter!"

By now this sweet Ruby was bent over she was

laughing so hard! I mean it *was* hysterical!! She was so busted!!

Grabbing my cell phone and quickly maneuvering it I was able to show her a picture of my beautiful little *African* princess named Ruby!

Her eyes were wide when she saw my Ruby. I giggled as I nearly shouted, "I told you!! I told you!! You didn't believe me!! She is just as beautiful as you are! Look at her!" Ruby was laughing loudly and nodding her head in agreement. Yes, my Ruby was just as beautiful as she was!!

It was a wonderful exchange as Dwight and I shared about our precious little miracle Ruby. We were able to show her that first emaciated picture of when Emma had found her and that led way to a beautiful discussion about the joys of adoption. As it turned out, this Ruby had always dreamed of adopting and we loved telling her to go for it!

Before long, by God's miraculous grace, even though the hospital was full and we had been told there likely wouldn't be a room that day, a room opened up on the 5th floor. I was thrilled. It was at the very end of the hall and my heart literally sighed as I entered it. It was the prettiest hospital room I had ever been in. Truly.

Settling into my new room, Dwight kept Liberty and our five marrieds in the loop through our family chat. I slept and slept as they pumped IV fluids that merely watered my very sick body. There is no medication for a desperately sick Hepatitis A liver! One just has to "ride it out" and with the four autoimmune diseases that I struggle with, the ride was proving to be bumpier than most.

Graham (who is often able to work from home when needed) headed right over to the house to help take care of the kids. Liberty is a very capable young woman but reinforcements are always good with a big old pile like ours! Knowing the kids were being well cared for was so good for my soul. I could rest well.

The first night Graham's pastor, Tim, came to pray for me along with one of Graham's friends, David (who had brought chicken wings for Dwight's dinner). It was such a tender time.

As I prepared to go to sleep for the night, Dwight mentioned that things were really serious with my liver. He said that he had been talking to Graham and that Graham was very concerned. At that point Dwight began to well with tears and said that Graham was wondering where he should go to get tested because he was ready to see if he was a match and would gladly donate part of his liver.

Our son's selfless love for me was hard to comprehend and I started to cry. As parents we have spent years caring for our kids and rarely are we given an opportunity to learn that they are willing to make such a sacrificial decision on our behalf. I started to wonder why I would need part of Graham's liver and although it may seem difficult to understand, I really was too sick to ask questions - until a couple of days later.

Come and hear, all you who fear God,
and I will tell what he has done for my soul.
Psalm 66:16

Chapter 21

Astoundingly Faithful

Three days later my two Liver Transplant Specialists came in together to see me. In the ER we had met Dr. B. She was so kind and had actually researched (on her own) the best essential oils for nausea to diffuse because she had noticed my diffuser going. I confess I was pretty tickled when person after person entered my room and commented that it was the best smelling room in the entire hospital!

Anyway, on Friday, Dr. M, the lead Liver Transplant Specialist was with Dr. B. We had met Dr. M a couple of days earlier, but when I saw them walk in together I actually thought, "This looks more serious."

When I had first met Dr. M he had wondered where I had grown up because he could tell from my accent that we were from the same area! As it turns out, we had actually grown up not far from each other in Buffalo, New York. It was a pleasure to talk with him about favorite eats, familiar places and also realize that we both share a love for the city of Buffalo, minus the snow and cold! We laughed as we agreed that any day in Phoenix heat was better than ever seeing a snowflake again!

This particular day though, Dr. M brought up Buffalo again and we talked for a minute about the blizzard of 1977. So after talking about Buffalo for a bit, Dr. M began.

He explained that my liver numbers had plateaued since I arrived at the hospital – they had not gone down at all. This meant that things were even more serious than the first day. They were extremely concerned that at any moment my liver situation "would go south" and I would need to be put on a Liver Transplant list.

Dr. M also explained that although Graham was more than willing to be tested as a possible match to give me part of his liver, because of my health, I would need a full liver.

It was then that the reality of what I was facing hit me! I had not suspected that this actually meant that I could die. **Dr. M explained that all my liver numbers meant that I was in Acute Liver Failure!**

Dr. B then explained something else. When I had arrived at the hospital that first night, after having the first blood work done, the tall ER doctor had phoned her in the middle of the night to say that he had a patient with ALT and AST numbers at or over 4,000. Dr. B told us that her first question to the ER doctor was, "Is she in a coma?" The ER doctor told her that I was talking, coherent and definitely not in a coma! She went on to tell us that with numbers like mine, they were stunned that I was not in a coma.

I now understood that it was completely miraculous and that only God had preserved my life! Yes, I was very sleepy, but I was lucid and very much awake. How grateful I am for His miraculous protection over me.

After Dr. M and Dr. B left my room, Dwight told me that Dr. B had actually told him all this in the ER hall the first day. After she explained how serious my situation was, with Missy visiting me, he had taken a walk to call each of our grown kids and tell them that things were very serious and that my life was actually in jeopardy. While talking to them, each had wondered if they should make flight reservations and come immediately? Dwight told them that he thought they should wait while they all prayed together in earnest asking God to move the numbers down!

Dwight later told me that over the days I was in the

hospital he would have to leave to go for a walk to have some time to cry, as it all was just too overwhelming. He was so concerned that I would not make it.

So as he prayed for me, he knew he had to ask others to pray. Well, as the Lord would have it, for the last nine years I have had the joy of writing a blog. With a love for writing, I had merely started it as a journal of our family life so our kids could look back over the years and remember life together. I never aspired, dreamed, desired or hoped for anything else. It was only ever my thought that it would be our little big-family journal.

However, what God did with my blog reminds me of Proverbs 16:9 "Man plans his ways, but God directs his steps." His plan is always best and far exceeds our good idea! When we lost our little log home to the fire, God instantly propelled my quiet little blog around the world as people everywhere shared the story of our large family losing our home to a fire. The blog, PlaceCalledSimplicity.com has now had over 5 million hits! Who could have ever imagined? Not me, never, ever, not even in a million years!

So as I lay desperately sick, Dwight knew he needed to ask the blog world to pray for me. Most of my blog friends understand the power of prayer. They have seen God's mighty hand move for them and can confidently say that prayer changes things! I am also grateful to say

218

that many have become personal friends over the years! God has definitely blessed me far more than I've ever deserved and I sure love this sweet bunch of blog friends around the world!

That first full day in, Dwight had hopped on my blog and briefly asked blog friends around the world to pray. No doubt, these precious friends dove in full force as they asked friends, family, Bible studies and churches to pray! The first blog post Dwight wrote about my health had over 8,000 unique views! That's a whole lot of loving concern right there!

Now a couple of days had passed and after Dr. B and Dr. M left, this was the first that I really understood that I might be facing a liver transplant if I lived long enough to get one! As Dwight and I talked, I began to cry. I just hadn't realized how serious it was. I hadn't had a clue that I should have been in a coma when I arrived at the hospital. I hadn't understood that I might be facing death. And although I was completely overwhelmed with the Lord's goodness to me, I also now realized that I could be facing a liver transplant. In the back of my mind, I had reasoned a couple of days earlier when Dwight mentioned Graham's willingness, "I'm not really sure what they are talking about but if I ever did need a liver, Graham is willing to donate, he will be a match, and it will all work out." Now I had heard first hand from my Liver Transplant Specialist that I would need a full liver and I knew that that is not something that is just "pulled off the shelf."

Tears streaming down my cheeks, I asked Dwight, "What if I never get to finish **The Memorial Box**? I desperately wanted people to understand that they have to remember what God has done! They have to! *Remembering what He has done, allows them to trust Him!*"

As I spoke those very words, peace flooded my soul. The Lord had this. I did not need to fret, worry or fear. He had never failed me. Not once, not even for a split second. He had always been faithful. If I needed a full liver, He was more than capable of providing one!

Dwight felt he wanted to tell our blog friends and ask them to pray specifically about how serious things were. I agreed. He could share - but not too much, as I, myself, still needed to process the full reality of it all. Anyone paying attention would understand that he was trying to tell them that things were really, really, really serious! He went on and wrote a brief post.

That same day Emma called me from Uganda. She and the other kids had been texting Daddy all the time, but now she wanted to talk to me. She needed me to understand that although she wanted to come home the needs there were so great that she felt she couldn't. I told her I didn't want her coming home!! I knew that she was needed there and I truly understood with all my heart.

Emma also told me about a song that she had recently heard. She wanted me to hear it as it had ministered powerfully to her and she felt it would also minister to me. It was by Travis Greene.

Made a Way

Made a way
Don't know how but You did it
Made a way
Standing here not knowing how we'll get through this test
But holding unto faith You know that
Nothing can catch You by surprise
You got this figured out and You're watching us now
But when it looks as if we can't win
You wrap us in Your arm and step in
And everything we need You supply
You got this in control
And now we know that
You made a way
When our backs were against the wall
And it looked as if it was over
You made a way
And we're standing here
Only because You made a way
You made a way
And now we're here
Looking back on where we come from
Because of You and nothing we've done
To deserve the love and mercy You've shown
But Your grace was strong enough to pick us up
And You made a way...

As I lay listening to the powerful lyrics, tears began to fill my eyes. Yes, I definitely felt like my back was against the wall and there was nothing I could possibly do; I also knew that nothing is impossible with my Miracle-working, Mountain-moving, Awe-inspiring, Gasp-giving God! He had done more than the miraculous over my lifetime and He would be faithful, no matter how my liver situation turned out! Throughout this trial, my only heart's cry was to praise Him. I knew He was working on my behalf, either way!

While lying in my hospital bed, I was so overcome with awe for my ever-faithful-best-friend, I softly whispered, "Lord, my favorite word for you is *faithful*. You know that's the first word I whisper when I think of you, in fact you know I whisper it all day long (literally) to you, but *faithful* alone seems sorely inadequate to describe just how faithful you really are. What could I add to make it truly speak of how I feel? Every word I can think of is so 'blah', yet you are so faithful."

Instantly He whispered, "Astoundingly." I smiled. YES! That was perfect!

You, oh Lord you are ***astoundingly faithful!***

Together the words, "astoundingly faithful" were perfect to describe how I feel about my Savior!

And from that moment on, I began to whisper them all day long to Him. He is *astoundingly faithful* - even when we doubt, even when we struggle, even when we fear. He remains ***astoundingly faithful!***

I listened to Made a Way dozens of times that day, prayerfully declaring His ***astounding faithfulness*** as people all over the world prayed with us for my numbers to drop. "Though our backs are against the wall, when it looked like it was over, You wrap us in your arm and step in..." Little did we know He was, indeed, making a way!

In the wee hours of the next morning, our Abigail had loaded her three handsome little guys in her car in San Francisco and started heading to Phoenix. She was so concerned she had to see me! She would also graciously take over caring for her nine youngest siblings while Graham and Savannah flew to a wedding they were to be in (if they went, depending on my situation).

Over the days, precious friends came to the hospital and showered me with flowers, cards, and love! Friends around the world sent loving messages and left words of encouragement, scripture, prayers and blessings. Blog friends sent gift cards and gifts! I felt so overwhelmingly loved. I was humbled beyond words and in complete awe!

On the home front our church, Highlands, was also pouring out the love! They had asked for prayer for me on one of the church's Facebook pages and immediately there was an enormous showering of extreme love toward our family! They started a meal train and a steady stream of gluten free meals began! We were shocked! Who signs up to bring a gluten free meal for a pile of eleven? What was even crazier was that we live 40 minutes from our church. But the distance, our family size and the need for gluten free didn't matter; they were 'all-in' with ministering to our big pile of treasures! We were completely blown away!!

Savannah said the meals were incredible and such a blessing because it meant she didn't have to think about what to make in the midst of all the other concerns, nor did she have to grocery shop for dinner ideas.

If that wasn't enough, our church called Savannah to ask her to make a list of what we normally buy at Costco. Before long Missy and friends showed up with loads and loads of food for our big pile of treasures! Many had chipped in to make it possible. We were in awe!! They also brought a card with gift cards to our local supermarket. We have never, in all our lives, had a church love us so lavishly.

By God's miraculous grace, *the very next day*, Dr. B came in and announced that my numbers had each dropped by a thousand overnight! She was cautiously hopeful – they were at least moving in the right direction and had broken through the plateau! Praise the matchless name of our *astoundingly faithful* God!

Listen friends, God moved the numbers because He loves. It's not because I deserved to live. I didn't. I am a sinner just like everyone else. In my younger years, I did my share of not-so-nice things. Yet God in His great mercy lowered the numbers. He alone. There was nothing I have ever done to deserve His love and mercy, and nothing I could do to lower them myself. It was only Him.

The following day Dr. B and Dr. M came in together and announced that my numbers had again dropped another 1,000 points each!! We were thrilled! Although my bilirubin had risen substantially (which accounted for the sunflower-gold shade I was sporting), they explained that the bilirubin is the last to rise and the last to fall.

Although I still was very sleepy and food sounded gross, I was so relieved to hear that things were improving greatly.

Eight days after entering the hospital, I was released. I would have to go to be tested weekly until my liver numbers returned to normal. It ended up actually taking three months to return to normal. Dr. M told me, "Your liver has taken a serious hit, and it will likely take many months to feel back to normal." Once home I slept much of the time, surrounded now by our youngest nine, our oldest Abigail and her sweet three – all of who bring my heart continuous healing joy!

As I write this chapter I am still healing. I still get very tired but am slowly gaining my strength back.

I have listened to Made a Way probably over a thousand times now. It plays all day long and if it is not playing, I am singing it. As I wake in the night to use the restroom, it is playing in my head.

He alone made a way!

As I look back on the first paragraph of this chapter where I explained how I prayed for the Lord to show me what the last chapter would be, I re-write my words:

"I longed for the last chapter to be personal, unquestionably powerful while emphatically declaring the undeniable faithfulness of our magnificent God."

Friend, there is no doubt that my perilous liver journey was deeply personal, unquestioningly powerful and through it all I can emphatically declare the *astounding faithfulness* of our magnificent God.

Although it has been a very difficult journey, I would take it again because of how it felt to know that the God of the universe was sustaining me, continually moving on my behalf, orchestrating each situation, preparing each person I would encounter and reminding me of just how *astoundingly faithful* He was at every turn!

There is no doubt that my heart was at complete peace the entire journey (with the exception of the hour I learned how serious it was from Dr. B and Dr. M).

I emphatically declare that the peace I had throughout the journey was because my trust was firmly rooted in my astoundingly faithful best friend, Jesus! I am also 100% confident that my trust has been built over many years of both trials and joys because we have chosen to remember what He has done, by routinely placing symbolic trinkets in our Memorial Box. We have chosen a lifestyle of remembering His astounding faithfulness.

If you have not yet begun a **Memorial Box**, it's never too late to start! Ask God to remind you of what He has done – He will! Then place something in your box to remind you of that particular story!

Tell the stories! They will encourage your soul, uplift your heart and reassure those around you of just how *astoundingly faithful* our all-powerful God is.

My hospital bracelet is in our Memorial Box as a reminder of His astounding faithfulness throughout this very difficult trial.

Let us hold fast the confession of our hope without wavering, for He who promised is faithful.
Hebrews 10:23

Epilogue:

One day while working on **The Memorial Box,** I was struck with how God has completely fulfilled His promise, *"The best years of your life are ahead of you!"* That prophetic promise was spoken in November 2005. Since that day, the Lord has graciously brought the following treasures home during these years:

- 2007 Isaiah Samuel
- 2008 Elizabeth Mercy
- 2008 Elijah Mueller
- 2009 Jubilee Promise
- 2011 Ruby Grace
- 2012 Nehemiah Judson
- 2016 John Vernon
- 2016 Birdie Bonnie (Pearl)

God has done above and beyond all that we could think or ask, with the arrival of not seven, but eight more in 9 years. How I praise Him - He has been so very good to me!

JOIN US! *Changing the World One Child At A Time*!

Join a GO Team!!
You are invited to join my Dwight or Linny on a
GO Team to serve the Special Needs treasures in a
developing nation of Africa. Trips are led four times a
year: April, June, September/October and January.
Email: **Office@InternationalVoiceOfTheOrphan.com**
for more information or to request an application.

Sponsor:
Join us in sponsoring a special needs orphan at: *The
Gem Foundation in Uganda.*   The Gem Foundation
currently cares for 31 special needs Gems. You may
choose a child to sponsor @The Gem Foundation.com.

Feed and Care:
International Voice of the Orphan (IVO) is a 501c3 that
Dwight and Linny began in 2011 in response to the vast
needs we saw while leading mission teams. Our work is
sharply focused and can be found at *IVO.global*

Feed: Join IVO in feeding meals to orphans in Africa,
vulnerable street children in Africa and the largely
forgotten children of a leper colony in India. Since it's
inception IVO has fed over 700,000 meals to these three
groups of precious treasures.

Medical: Join IVO in providing medical care to orphans
& vulnerable children with families in developing
countries as well as medical care for the Gems at The
Gem Foundation.

To contact the author: aplacecalledsimplicity@yahoo.com

51223709R00131

Made in the USA
San Bernardino, CA
16 July 2017